TWO TO FOUR

FROM

9 TO 5

TWO TO FOUR

FROM

9 TO 5

THE ADVENTURES OF
A DAYCARE PROVIDER

JOAN ROEMER

AS TOLD TO

BARBARA AUSTIN

1817

HARPER & ROW, PUBLISHERS, New York

Grand Rapids, Philadelphia, St. Louis, San Francisco

London, Singapore, Sydney, Tokyo

FIRST EDITION

Designed by Alma Orenstein

Library of Congress Cataloging-in-Publication Data

Roemer, Joan.
  Two to four from 9 to 5: the adventures of a daycare provider/ Joan Roemer as told to Barbara Austin.
    p.   cm.
  ISBN 0-06-016085-3
  1. Roemer, Joan. 2. Child care workers—California—Oakland— Biography. 3. Family daycare—California—Oakland—Case studies. I. Austin, Barbara Leslie. II. Title.
HV859.018R64   1989
362.7'12'09—dc20   [B]   88-45904

---

89 90 91 92 93 AT/HC 10 9 8 7 6 5 4 3 2 1

To my children—John, Tim, Karen, and Laura
—in deep appreciation for making me a parent.

—Joan Roemer

To my parents—Maxine and Bill Linton
—in deep appreciation for giving me this
opportunity.

—Barbara Austin

Contents

Acknowledgments   ix

Prologue: Beginnings   1

PART ONE: Limitations   5

PART TWO: Marvels   71

PART THREE: Stew Babies   121

PART FOUR: Roots and Wings   279

Epilogue: A Special Christmas Party   292

Acknowledgments

The life of a book is not so different from the life of a child—fits and starts, two steps forward, one step back—but if you believe in the process and you accept the natural progression and regression, something wonderful can happen. I'd like to thank Phyllis Peacock and Don Margrof, who were there during the fits and starts in the beginning; Judie Landis for keeping me honest all the way along; the children and parents who I have had the privilege of knowing and loving all these years; my friend Linda Peterson for taking my early material to Barbara Austin; Barbara Akre, my sister, who is content to be Watson to my Sherlock—you know as well as I know you're the backbone, my much better half—I thank you for being so completely supportive to this book; and, lastly, Barbara Austin herself. Finally, I found someone to talk to who understood what I was trying to say, who could contain it and tell it in the way I always wanted it to be told. You did become me. And, Barbara—you have found a friend for life.
—Joan Akre Roemer

This book is a work of collaboration. I'd also like to thank Linda Peterson of Peterson, Skolnick and Dodge; Felicia Eth, my agent, for her great ideas; and Janet Goldstein, our editor at Harper & Row. She truly believes that "less is more" and she's right. And Leslie, for putting up with so much. Above all, I thank Joan Roemer for her generous heart, depth, superb memory, and, above all, for who she is—the real thing—one of the kindest, finest people I have ever known. Thank you for truly being my partner in this. May it read like the joy it was to write!

—Barbara Linton Austin

The children, families, and incidents presented on these pages are authentic. However, in order to protect the privacy of certain children and adults mentioned in this book, some names and identifying details have been changed. In some instances, we have created composites for the purpose of further disguising the identity of the individuals.

Prologue

Beginnings

I T SEEMS SUCH AN ORDINARY LIFE.

I live on a dead-end street in Oakland, California, in a three-story wooden house, and every day in my home I take care of other people's children. From 9 to 5, five days a week, forty-eight weeks a year, I watch over them with enormous care.

I am a daycare provider.

I say this with pride, compassion, and a well-exercised sense of humor. It is not an easy task being a provider. But I love what I do and, as with any work that is lifelong and life-enveloping, I find my own equilibrium in it. I am able to be with these children fully and take my comfort from them.

Once I had a dream that I was in the backseat of a car with four or five children and that they were chewing me alive. This is an understandable dream for a provider. Being with twelve children under the age of five on a daily basis is truly all-consuming. You can be eaten up. And some providers are. They find their houses—and lives—totally taken over by their daycare work, often reduced to living in one room at the back.

That stunted way of living is not for me. I love my home. It is my best friend. And I make it beautiful for my daycare children as I do for my own family and guests. Each week I have arranged a bouquet or two of fresh flowers. I have favorite things everywhere, and because they are not untouchable, the children are not attracted to them and prefer their own things. At first, people are often amazed at this. . . . "What a lovely home, Joan . . . and you take care of twelve toddlers?"

Yes. Other people's children share my life and my home and I am daily inspired by them. At the end of each day I know I have done something important. Sometimes, of course, it is only that I've survived the day! My sister, Barbara, who has worked with me hand in glove for fifteen years, shares this love.

Indeed, I believe what happens in my house is important and worth sharing—but it is not because I am a woman who poetically loves other people's children. I don't really. I am no different from any mother, who, to a large extent, can take or leave other people's children but adores her own. I didn't get into this work because of some romance. I certainly wouldn't have stayed in it all these years. And, frankly, I don't trust people very much who go around saying, "I just love kids, don't you?"

No, I am my father's child to a great extent. I believe in an idea. My father believed in ideas. He was a poor man from South Dakota who did everything he could to better himself. He read *The New Yorker* every week; he bought my mother, a farm girl, clothes out of Peck & Peck; he played the trombone in a Dixieland band in little towns all over the country to put himself through a good college. And, after he graduated, he was a crusader who fought for an idea, and because of it, was destroyed, but that is another story.

Why I am here, and take such extraordinary care with the children left to me each day, is because I believe in that old idea that we can change the way we are in the world through our children. I believe that we are not merely fostering children here, but, rather, helping create wonderful adults. And that my being with children in the way that I am, matters. It matters a great deal. I began my daycare out of this belief.

When I started fifteen years ago, the world of daycare was very different. At that time, there was little interest, support, and knowledge about it. Different from nursery schools, which were primarily for enrichment a few times a week, daycares were used every day by divorced, single, and financially strapped women as a place to leave their children while they worked. Today daycares are used by the well-off and the poor, whether the mother works or not. And they have become a national issue and necessity.

Fifteen years ago, like the issue of daycare itself, I was isolated. I assumed too much responsibility. So this story is as much about marvels that happen here every day as it is about the process of how I discovered who I was in this work as I defined my own limitations.

It has been a long process. When I began, I had four teenage children, I had just completed three years' work in an experimental classroom in the Berkeley public school system, and I was eager to open my own school. Since I had trained in a daycare in the fifties while going to college and been fortunate enough to take seminars in early childhood development as I trained, I felt prepared for the task. I was also forty then, married and full of energy and new ideas.

Today, fifteen years later, I am fifty-five, a grandmother of nine, still full of energy and ideas, but with a much deeper theoretical and practical base. All during these years, I have studied, sought direction, and developed. And I know now that at every moment of every day I am doing good work with these children. But in the beginning, I certainly did not know this.

Like everyone in my life, you'll get your fill of my ideas, but, above all, I want you to meet some of my children, past and present—those who have made this life of mine so extraordinary, day after ordinary day.

PART ONE

Limitations

1

Little Al Capone

TWELVE YEARS AGO, this particular morning began like any other. It was fall so there was a light feathery drizzle outside. The smell of blueberry waffles that the children had had for breakfast was still in the air. And Emily and her grandmother had finally arrived. Her grandmother slowly pulled her to school every day, rain or shine, in a red wagon. They always took the same route so they could notice which flowers bloomed and then faded and then which ones bloomed again. Today Emily arrived sitting, full of delight, in the center of the wagon holding a small orange umbrella above her head.

Each morning Sandy, my beloved and well-trained golden retriever, greeted every child by lying very flat on the floor and wagging her whole backside, whining softly. When an arriving child knelt down to pat her hello, she would lick and wiggle all over, keeping her head low. When the greeting was over, Sandy lumbered into the playroom with the child and settled herself until the front door opened and the next child arrived. Then she would jump up and the procedure would begin anew.

Sandy had just completed her morning's work and lay beside me in front of the fire. Ten children sat around me in a semicircle sipping from mugs of hot cocoa as I read to them.

And Jeffie was laughing again. We were reading his favorite, *Peter Pan,* and every time we got near a certain page where, in this version, Smee steals the cannonball from Captain Hook so he can't shoot Peter Pan, Jeffie would start to giggle. He would try to contain himself by covering up his face and pacifier with his hands, but as we got nearer and nearer to the page he couldn't do it. So he was laughing again, laying back on the rug, almost spilling his mug of cocoa as he laughed. He laughed so hard his pacifier shot out of his mouth and flew across the room. Around him were his favorite things of the moment. He loved everything green so near him was a rubber frog, the "Sesame Street" lamppost, and a green airplane.

"Jeffie!" I was saying through my laughter, because he always got me started. "We can't hear the story. We've still got two pages left before we even get to that part—" when I heard it. Sandy pricked up her ears, too, for over and above Jeffie's uncontrollable laughter, we could hear the new boy screaming.

I laid the book down, got up, and went to the window to see Timmy D. in diapers, wearing a football helmet and screaming at the top of his lungs as he clutched at his tall father, begging him, in indecipherable sobbing syllables, not to leave him.

"Babadadawannawanna!" he screamed.

Finally, his father, in his own skewed but effective way, not bothering to pick him up, but grabbing him and holding him by his upper arm, carried him, nearly at arm's length, all the way up our front stairs.

Timmy, meanwhile, still screaming, was desperately trying to get hold of his father's face with his other arm. His father was able to open our front door by kicking it wide with his foot. He then deposited his son in the entryway. Turning, barely saying a word to me, he rushed out the door, slamming it behind him. This was the beginning of Timmy's second week with us.

Timmy jumped up, ran to the closed door sobbing, ''Babadadadawanna,'' again and banging his fists against it. But before Sandy and I could get near him, he turned, saw Jeffie still laughing on the playroom floor, his stomach vulnerable and exposed, and ran across the room, throwing himself upon him, kicking and pummeling him with his fists. Jeffie, in sheer terror, hit him on the back with his green airplane. I dove in, tearing them apart, trying to pull Timmy off Jeffie. He was so strong, even at two, that he almost knocked me over. He was willing to do anything to get back at Jeffie for hitting him with the plane.

"Barbara!" I called out to my sister and daycare partner. She was still in the kitchen cleaning up the children's breakfast. She came running, drying her hands on a dish towel, and she took Jeffie to the rocking chair in the other playroom.

Meanwhile, I tried to talk to Timmy. I also tried not to get hurt myself because he was hitting me in the face and kicking me in the chest. Finally, I just put him back on the floor.

He tore at me again, banging his football helmet against my chin. Finally, I had him as far away from me as I could keep him, holding him down on the floor with my foot on his back. I couldn't even look at him because I didn't know what to do with this screaming, incoherent little boy. This was the third year of our operation and never before had I witnessed such a violent tantrum.

Barbara tried to call his parents. There was no answer any place—not at home or at his father's or mother's office. Finally, worn down, he stopped thrashing, screaming, and hitting. I took him in my arms and said, "Timmy, you're so upset."

"Blupbub up!" he said, pushing me away.

His father finally drove by at noon to pick him up. I said, "Timmy, your father's here," and he ran right out the door and down the stairs. His father opened the car door. His older brother, John, aged five, was in the backseat. Timmy climbed in the front door and up on the seat, sitting very close to his dad, but he didn't say a word.

The car had already started when I leaned in his window, saying, "Anthony, I want to talk to you. I want to tell you how upset Timmy's been all morning."

"We're on our way to get an ice cream cone. We're going to talk it over."

"Well, I was wondering what had happened because Tim's been unusually upset this morning."

He looked up at me and said, "He and John had some altercation about a piggy bank," and then he put his Buick in gear and drove off.

I stared after them. Some altercation about a piggy bank.

I expected some concern, some interest, but it was clear, whatever it was, Timmy's father didn't want to discuss it with me.

2

Jennifer's Dilemma

ONE DAY JENNIFER SAID TO ME, "Could I live with you?" She was three and had been coming to daycare for about six months.

"No, Jen, children live with their parents," I said as I wiped the perspiration off my upper lip. I was cooking carrots on our gas stove, getting lunch ready. The rest of the children were with Barbara, either playing inside the house or outside in the enclosed play yard.

"Karen and Laura live with you."

"Right," I said as I carefully ladled some turkey juice into a pan for gravy. "They're my children and I'm their mother. They live with me just like you live with your mother."

"Who else lives in a family?"

"Like what?" I turned and looked at her standing by the stove in front of the stools. "You mean other family members like Grandma and Grandpa, or what?"

She was standing on one leg, furrowing her forehead. "Yes, like that, Joanie." Her doll hung by one lank arm at her side. "Maybe I could be a family member?" She looked up at me hopefully.

"I just have Karen and Laura living here now as members of the family, Jen." I put down the ladle, looked at her, and said, "You know, you and I are special, like a family to each other. And I couldn't love you any more than I do now, wherever you live." I put my hand on her head. "You've spent the night, you can do that again." Then I smiled. "Jen, everyone has a family. You and your mom and your dad. You live together as a unit." I put the fingers of two hands together, making a unit. "What would your family do without you?"

"Oh," she said, seeming to understand as she walked out, swinging her doll behind her.

A few days later, Jen came up to me in the yard as I was sitting on the bench fixing Cindy's braid. "Joanie, people have servants."

I looked at her.

"I saw it on TV. There are maids and maids that are men who tell the women maids what to do."

"Oh," I said, twisting on the rubber band. "What show were you watching?"

"I can be a maid and live with you! If I make the beds and do work, I don't have to be a family member to live with you. I know maids can do this, Joanie, because I saw it. So can I do that?"

"No, Jennifer." I patted Cindy's back as she jumped off my lap and the bench and ran back into the sandbox. "I am not employing servants at this time." I lifted her up and put her next to me on the bench as I watched the other children play. "Debra! Jonathan! Don't throw sand. Leave the sand in the sandbox." I turned back to her. "Jen, you and I are friends," I said. "Very special friends. Sometimes it feels like

I'm your grandma or mom, I know. Maybe you even feel that
I would love you more if you really were my daughter. Or
maybe it's just because you want to live in my home and sit
on my bed and watch color TV and have popcorn every
night. . . ."

"I don't want your old TV," she said laughingly.

"Jen." I put my hand on each side of her perky face.
She had curly ringlets of black hair and very dark shiny eyes.
"What we have is what we have. I love you and you love me
and we're special to each other, even as special, in some
ways, as Mom and daughter. But Mom and daughter we're
not, and we can't change that."

"Okay, okay," she said, sounding not very disappointed, as she jumped off the bench and then off to play on
the bars with her friends.

Meanwhile, Jennifer started throwing fits every time Loretta, her mother, came to take her home. Here Loretta was,
in the midst of all the other children absolutely delighted to
be picked up, running all over themselves to be with Mom
and Dad, and Jennifer either completely ignored her or would
hit or kick at her when she tried to get Jennifer's coat on.
Loretta was becoming increasingly concerned with her
daughter's antics.

Finally, Jen cornered my seventeen-year-old daughter
Karen as she was coming home from high school. "Bye, Jed,"
she said to her boyfriend as she waved and came in the front
door. She turned and there was Jennifer standing in the doorway, holding a blond-haired doll in one hand and the dirty
hem of her favorite "dress-up" skirt in the other.

"Are you leaving soon to live somewhere else now that
you're grown-up?"

Karen stopped, looked down, smiled, and started to walk
on up the stairs.

But Jen got between Karen and the stairs. "Will Joanie be lonely when you leave?" she asked, waving her doll in the air.

"Oh, I don't think so," Karen said as she walked around Jen and started up the stairs to her room. She had no idea what Jen was getting at.

"Well, if you want to move I want you to know it's okay with Joanie."

Karen stopped on the stairs and began to laugh. "Well," she said, turning around. "Is she trying to get rid of me or what?"

Jennifer, very seriously, covered part of her mouth with her hand and whispered loudly, "I think she is."

3

A Monster Invades
the Daycare

EANWHILE, TIMMY CONTINUED to be a challenge. He had a way of walking into the playroom and standing there in his Kung Fu T-shirt and football helmet, looking around. The other children would scurry away. They knew that look. We called it "Timmy's moods."

We're in for it, I'd think.

He had an olive complexion and very dark brown eyes and if he'd come to school in a mood his eyes would seem to darken and black circles would appear under them. After his look around the playroom, he'd stick out his lower lip and pounce on whoever was nearest him, usually Jeffie.

All Timmy had to do was make a sudden jerk and we'd be running. Often, his jerk would only mean he was going after a ball. It would be funny to watch our fits and starts. Barbara and I were always tense and on duty with this child.

But no matter how fast either of us was, Timmy would

always get in a couple of punches before I could separate him from his victim. Then he would turn on me and start punching and kicking me. Now it was I who was trying desperately to push him away.

Meanwhile, Jeffie would need comforting and Barbara would take him into the other room and rock him in the rocking chair. Our dog Sandy, the most guilt-ridden dog imaginable, would need comforting also, because whenever a child cried she always thought it was her fault.

"It's okay, Sandy," Barbara would say, "Jeffie will be all right."

"Yeh, old girl," Jeffie would say out of the side of his pacifier, "Timmy hurt me," and then he would cry all over again as he comforted Sandy.

At the same time, Timmy would still be hitting and kicking me. I would have trouble protecting myself because this little boy was so strong. "Stop it," I said. "You're all right. It's all over, Timmy, just calm down." While I ducked his blows, some of the other children would come over to see what was going on, and he'd try to punch them out too.

So I would end up taking him into the kitchen to get away from everyone else. I'd set him in the middle of our large round kitchen table so he couldn't reach me to hit or kick, and also, to keep him from dashing into the other room to get back at Jeffie.

At that time, I didn't know much about tantrums or two-year-olds. During our first two years, we had taken only three- and four-year-olds. All I knew was that I hated what I was doing. I wanted him to stop misbehaving. But nothing was working and I was getting angrier and angrier and more and more panicky at the same time. I couldn't seem to find a solution and I wasn't sure I ever would.

It was as if a monster invaded the playroom when Timmy was seized with a fury. Five minutes before he would be totally involved in a story I was reading. Then he might nonchalantly get up, go over, and start playing with blocks as I continued. If a couple of blocks happened to fall down, he would grab them and throw them at me or anyone else.

By the fifth tantrum of the day, I would reach a point where I wanted to scream, "I don't want to have to deal with you every hour on the hour. I want to be able to read to the children, I want Jeffie to laugh again, I want everyone to enjoy their play. I want us to do pleasant things!"

One day, my friend Carol Washburn came early to pick up her little girl, Tina. She found me in the kitchen as usual, trying to corral a black-eyed, screaming, football-helmeted Timmy in the middle of my kitchen table.

"What are you?" she asked. "A lion tamer?"

"Close," I said. She was an expert in working with emotionally disturbed children. "But tamer I'm not."

Finally, he calmed down. As I took him back to the playroom, she asked, "What in the world are you going to do with him?" She knew that more than one parent had already complained about Timmy's interaction with their child and that some were beginning to get worried about their children's safety here.

I turned and looked at her, all high heels and chunky silver jewelry. I was filthy dirty as usual at the end of the day. "Carol," I said exhaustedly, "I haven't a clue."

4

Jennifer's Dilemma Persists

IS KAREN REALLY LEAVING?" Jennifer asked.

I was sitting at my desk in the small playroom right before naptime. I said, "She hasn't mentioned it to me. Has she talked with you about it?"

Leaning on the desk, she shook her shiny curls. "Just a little bit." She rubbed her doll back and forth, back and forth on the desk surface. "She wants to know if you would be lonely if she leaves." She looked up from her doll and at me with those glistening black eyes. "Will you?"

"Well," I got up from behind the desk to call the children. "You tell her that I won't be lonely because we can arrange to see each other, maybe every day."

The next day, her mother stopped me. "Joan," she asked, "what's going on?"

By this time, it turned out, Jen was refusing to eat dinner

at home with her family. Each afternoon, around 5:00, she'd been asking for something to eat, so I suggested that I stop that afternoon snack to see if that would help. Not long after, Jen refused to change from the long "dress-up" skirts that she and her friends wore during the day into what she called her "going-home" clothes. So I tried to see to it that she changed clothes before her mother arrived. Needless to say, Loretta was becoming increasingly hurt by all this and thought perhaps Jen was angry with her for leaving her each day.

Though I didn't quite know what was so difficult for Jen, I could easily relate to her mother. One afternoon I said to her, "You know, I can understand why this is worrisome for you." We sat down for a few moments on the back deck as Jennifer continued to play with her friends. "I know that it was for me when I picked up my children from spending the night at my mother's house and they were unhappy to leave." I laughed. "They were disappointed to see me come for them! But when we got home we all settled in happily again." She nodded, for that was her experience with Jennifer too. "Perhaps it's more about switching gears," I said. "Leaving a happy place and having to start up again at home. It seems like a big transition at the end of the day."

She smiled, looking around her at the two swings, the dome climber, the huge sandbox, the cars, the basketball hoop. Then she said, "You know, we chose your place. Harold and I looked at, oh, I don't know—*five* different day-cares—and we knew yours was right because we both wanted to come here ourselves!"

"Yes," I said, as I took her out through the kitchen. "I remember you telling me that." I smiled at her. "You're doing just fine, Loretta. You really are. *Every parent feels guilty.*"

"They do?"

"No matter what they do—leave the child with a nanny, take them here, take them there—they never feel it's enough."

"Oh."

"Even women who stay *home* with their children feel guilty for not being good enough at-home mothers!"

"Oh," she said again. She glanced across the hall where Jennifer was laughing with her friends. "When do you suppose it will get easier?" she asked.

"I don't know," I said honestly. "But let's just see where she's going with this."

A few days later, Jen asked, as I was in the kitchen cleaning up after snacktime, "Can I use the broom?"

"Sure, it's behind the door." I put another dish in the drainer.

A few minutes went by.

"Now can I have a washrag?"

"Not a wet one." I pointed. "The dry ones are in the drawer."

When she came back later to put it away, I asked, "What have you been doing?"

"Practicing." She held her doll by one arm and brushed one of its arms on the floor.

"Practicing what?"

"To be a maid."

I laughed and shook my head. "You don't give up easily."

"No."

5

Language

"TIMMY," TINA WASHBURN SAID. "What this?"

"Abadababa."

"What's that?" Tina, Jennifer, and Amy looked at each other. They had decided to teach Timmy to talk.

"Abadaba*baba*," he said, frustrated, pointing over in Amy's direction.

"Aba-daba-baba?" Tina said. She had just turned four. "This?" She pointed at a teddy bear.

"No, he means this!" Amy held up a cassette tape player.

"This!" Jennifer cried, jumping on a set of blocks.

"Abadababababub!" And he threw himself at the three of them, butting them with his football helmet, his arms going like propellers.

"Timmy!" I cried, already there.

*   *   *

You see, Timmy couldn't talk. He could say Mamama and Dadada, but everything else came out in nearly all nonsense syllables. If he wanted me, he'd say, "Inainadaboodada," very rapidly. He'd look at a boat and say, "Babababa." He always used so many more syllables than were needed, always said very fast.

In fact, this is a bit how his mother sounded to me. Jackie always talked so quickly that I could usually understand only every other word. She'd come to get him, park her car by banging the cars in front and in back, run in, and start a very fast conversation with one of the other parents. Meanwhile, Timmy, with his nonsense syllables, would be begging to go home. I realized he felt he needed to keep going like a motor when he talked to keep one's attention. His father, on the other hand, who was already teaching this little two-year-old karate stances, said very little.

Timmy would be terribly frustrated trying to get us to understand. He would take Barbara or me around by the arm and point to what he needed. You see, to him all this rapid nonsense syllable language made sense. Every object had a name—it just wasn't the one we used.

One day, about three months after he first arrived, he came over to me while I was sitting on one end of the couch watching the children. He seemed to be in a very mellow mood. His eyes were a lighter brown and had none of their usual dark rings. He had on his football helmet as usual and a diaper. He knelt beside me. I turned my head toward him and he reached out and took my face in both his hands, and looking straight into my eyes, he said, "Joan."

"Timmy," I answered, without thinking.

It took a moment to realize what had just happened. . . . He had said my name. "Barbara!" I called. "Barbara."

This began a very long and, for me, harrowing process.

Timmy would sit near me or on my lap and stare at me intently with those dark little eyes as he got each word out. If I diverted my eyes for any reason, he would grab my face with both his hands and force my attention back.

What he worked on first were syllables. He had to have the exact number. Sometimes he'd call me "Goan" or "Moan" or "Toan" but he began to get the syllables correctly. We'd be sitting outside on the bench under the mimosa tree, and as the buds fell on us, he'd cock his head as he spoke to me. He was deliberately trying to slow down and listen to what he was saying.

After he got the syllables, he worked on getting the sound right. What he was doing, of course, was teaching himself to speak. And he needed a listener.

Once I saw him holding onto Sandy's face with both hands, talking to her. Oh, good, I thought, he's using the dog. Sandy's so much more patient than me. "Tandy," he was saying. "Nandy."

And it would take him so long to say something. He would be talking to me when I'd look over to see a child teetering on the swing and he would grab my face and bring it back to his eyes and he would stare at me: "I . . . a . . . a . . . a . . . *want* . . . a . . ." and then he'd point and point. And if I dared look over in that direction, he'd pull my face back, trying to get the word. "Aaa . . ."

I'd say hopefully, "Amy?"

He'd say, "Memememe." Then he'd shake his head because he'd know that wasn't right.

I'd say, "Amy."

And he'd say, "Mememe," and smile because he thought he got it right. And if he thought it so, I wouldn't say a word.

If he wanted to tell me something—like how his older brother did this or that—it would take fifteen minutes. And nothing is *that* interesting. One time he told the whole story of his birthday party, and I listened to every single word, as he held my face and as his eyes were riveted on mine. One candle . . . two candles. . . . Fortunately, he wasn't very old.

*   *   *

The months went by, and he began to be able to tell me whole stories. One day he came in with one black eye. Three days later, he came in with the other eye black. I was talking to his mother the next day and I mentioned that even though the football helmet he loved and wore all the time was good protection, he was still hurting himself. "That bad knot by his eye disturbs me, Jackie," I said.

"You know, Joan," she said very quickly, "you know, boys play so rough."

She thought Timmy got the knot by tripping over his shoelaces and falling down. Or perhaps he and John were fighting again, she really didn't know.

The next day, I sat down beside Timmy on the floor in the playroom. "Timmy," I asked, "how'd you get that black eye?"

He climbed into my lap and told me, laboriously, how his older brother had pushed him down while he was running. I felt for him. His life was rage and battles here, fights with his brother and, from what I could tell, little supervision at home. I felt in a quandary. He needed my help, but I didn't know what to do.

I remember one Monday morning he came in with one shoe on and one shoe off. That didn't mean anything until I noticed there were Band-Aids on his foot and he was limping.

"Timmy," I said. "What's the matter with your foot?"

"I hurt," he said.

I got down on my knees to examine his foot but he quickly limped away. He didn't want me to look at it. I followed him and he started hitting me. I picked him up and took him out to the kitchen table. Finally he let me look at it.

What I saw stung me: he had two huge sores on his foot. One was already infected.

He was watching me. "Timmy," I said, "your feet hurt so much because they're infected."

And I took him in my arms and carried him to the sink. I filled it with warm Epsom salt water and let him play with boats while his feet soaked. He sat in the water and picked up a little blue motorboat, and then he started to cry.

"I so—*angry*," he said. "John . . . push . . . me. . . ." It took a long time for him to tell it, but I got the story.

He had been riding down the sidewalk in front of his house on his Hot Wheels bike. His brother had pushed him faster than he could go so he put his feet out to stop himself and he scraped the skin off the tops of both of his feet. He'd finally run into a tree to stop.

Barbara and I traded off taking him to the sink for warm soaks and fresh bandages. He loved all the attention. Sometimes I would sit in a chair next to the sink and we would talk about how he felt. "It must have been horrible to be going faster than you could steer," I said. "And it must hurt so—your feet must have hurt terribly."

"No . . ." he would say. "After. . . ." And he'd mean that they didn't hurt while John was pushing him, only after. "John . . . mean." And he would rant and rave about how mean John was. I thought about that. And then what it must be like having Timmy for a brother. And then I would imagine the frustration Timmy must have felt before he could begin to talk about his feelings.

Meanwhile, his father continued teaching him karate. I talked to his mother about it. I said, "Timmy comes into the playroom and takes karate stances now, Jackie."

"I know," she said, looking at me and then away. She reminded me of Tim, so small and energetic, with those same dark lively eyes. "I've been worried about it too." She laughed. "Even though I'm a therapist and seem to have helpful advice for other people, I'm really at a loss to understand what's going on with Timmy." Then she looked at me directly and said, "I don't know what to think, Joan."

I talked to her about what I saw as Timmy's burgeoning vulnerability. I told her how he had cried in the tub over his hurt feet and his brother. "I feel we might try to nurture his soft feelings," I said. "Perhaps this isn't the time for karate."

She nodded.

I said, "Do you know he's teaching himself to talk?"

She said, "Well, he's sure working on it," and laughed.

"He's determined that we're all going to understand what he has to say," I said, and laughed too.

The more attention I gave Timmy, the more he needed. And all the while he persisted in his tantrums and more and more parents were noticing. Sometimes they would be there when he would leap on a child; other times, their own children told them. I would say in response to their fears, "If your child were having a hard time, I would be there for him or her, just like I am for Timmy. Barbara and I are very attentive. No one is in danger from Timmy. Let us deal with it with the children—they love him, you know, and they're learning, too, from Timmy's frustrations."

Until one day I got hurt. And I felt I couldn't go on.

6

The Beginning
of the End

THIS AFTERNOON WE WERE COMING, as a group, into the house from out-of-doors. Timmy and Jeffie ran on ahead and the others were close behind. Suddenly, movement stopped. I ran through the group to see what was going on. Timmy and Jeffie were on the floor in the laundry room, screaming and hitting and kicking each other.

"My pluggie! He stole my pluggie!" Jeffie screamed, grabbing for his pacifier. He had two constantly in hand. No one stole Jeffie's pluggie without a fight.

As I squeezed on through the back door to get at these two boys, I hit my elbow on the door frame. I stood there a moment, paralyzed with pain.

As I reached down to grab a part of each of them, Timmy kicked me full in the mouth with the tip of his shoe. He hadn't meant to, I knew this, but I was already in pain from banging myself on the door. In a rush of current pain and frustration coupled with a great deal of past pains and frustration, I grabbed them both, and with fantasies of doing them bodily harm, I let out exactly what I was thinking: "I am so sick and tired of you, Timmy! I wish you weren't even here."

He stopped hitting Jeffie immediately and looked up at me, stunned.

There. It was said. I didn't care if it was a real blow to him, he had heard. "Give him back his pluggie, Timmy D.! Right now!"

I tore it out of his hand which was unnecessary, for he was handing it over. I gave the pluggie to Jeffie, who whimpered away.

"Every time I come to rescue you," I said to Jeffie's backside, "I get hurt!"

Guilty now at my outburst on top of the pain and tiredness, I was becoming angrier. I said to Timmy, "You kicked me in the mouth, Timmy Duranto! Why do you fight all the time? Everyone is sick to death of you and your fights! Especially *me!* Now get into the other room and be quiet in there. If I decide I want to feed you, I'll call you to lunch, but don't you dare come back in here until I do!"

The crisis was over but all my anger was not spent. I told the other children, "Get in the kitchen and sit down. I don't want to hear a peep out of any of you until lunch is over."

They were all very quiet and watched me with big eyes. This was new behavior on my part. Barbara was quiet too as she washed hands and faces. I began to help with washing up. Not a sound from the playroom from Timmy. Jeffie was vigorously sucking on his pluggie and watching with huge eyes from the corner of the small table, waiting to see what would happen next.

I was feeling bad about my behavior now, but I didn't know how to break the silence. I knew I didn't want to say anything nice to anybody because I was still mad. My lip was swollen and it felt funny. I began to feel sorry for myself. I thought, Be careful now, you don't want to start crying on top of everything else.

A few more uncomfortable moments went by. Finally, I heard Barbara say, "My, my, we've had quite a morning, haven't we? Jeffie and Timmy had a fight and Joanie gets a fat lip. Ha. Ha. Well, that's too bad but we all get a bump here and there and from time to time. Now Tina, what would you like on your plate?"

This allowed me to say, "I'll pass out the milk."

Barbara said to me, "If you'll serve, I'll go get Timmy."

Bless Barbara's heart, it was over. But as far as I was concerned, Timmy could stay in the other room forever.

7

Jennifer's Dilemma Concludes

ONE DAY JENNIFER came up to me in the kitchen after snacktime. "My dolly wants to spend the night here."

"Okay," I said as I opened the trash bin and put the apple cores inside.

"Every night," she said, flopping her curly head up and down.

"Okay," I said and closed the cupboard door.

She took me upstairs to my bedroom. She stood in the door, cradling her doll, and carefully looked all over my room. Should she place her under the chair? Should it be under the table or by the fireplace? She dropped to her knees and checked under my bed. She went downstairs and found a box. She lined the box with her blanket. She even found a small toy pillow. Carefully she wrapped the doll in the blanket and tucked her in. She went downstairs to the hall closet and got a broom. As I waited, she swept under the bed, and

30

then, kissing her dolly, she put her cradle carefully under my bed.

"There!" she said, wiping her hands.

On Friday, she asked, "Can my dolly stay the weekend?"

"Of course," I said. I was standing outside on the deck.

So before going home, she carefully tucked her under the bed in my room.

Monday morning, holding the doll in her arms, she asked me, as I was fixing the wing on Jeffie's green airplane, "Did dolly sleep well?"

"Oh yes," I said. "Like a log."

"Did she have a good time? Did she eat well?"

"Oh yes," I said. "Like a horse."

"Did she enjoy her bath?"

I was going to say, like a duck, but I resisted. "Ah huh," I said, and I looked up from the airplane and smiled. Then I glanced away. "Timmy D.!" I called. "That is Danny's car right now. Let him have his turn."

Once Jennifer began to leave her doll here, it became easier for her to go home in the evenings. Jen would leave her dolly every night and every day she would want to know every detail about how her doll spent her time with me. "What TV shows did she watch? Did you have popcorn? Did she have any scary dreams?" Then one Saturday as I was vacuuming under my bed I found her doll. Jennifer had forgotten to pick her up.

"Don't you want to see how dolly is?" I asked her on Monday.

"Oh. Oh yeah," she said, sighing, and trudged upstairs without enthusiasm.

That night when her mother came to pick her up, she mentioned that Jen's behavior at home had pretty much returned to normal.

At the end of the week, Jen ran up to me out in the yard, and putting her hand lightly on my arm, said, "I'm sorry, Joanie, but my dolly doesn't want to spend the weekend here. She wants to be home."

"Okay," I said and smiled.

8

Rolph

'M NOT GOING TO CARE SO MUCH about Timmy anymore, I had decided the week before as I carefully listened and followed each child's lunch order the day of Timmy and Jeffie's fight. As my anger diminished, I began to even feel hopeful. Perhaps I can get some relief, I thought.

The evening after the fight I asked Barbara to oversee Timmy at least half the time. And after just a few days of relief I felt positively energetic. I was amazed, looking back, at how exhausted I had become. I even had enough energy to do something I had not done for a long time. I invited my friend Carol Washburn over for dinner. I prepared baked chicken with onions, carrots, and new potatoes, set the table, and arranged my favorite flowers—wild pink roses that smell like sweet pepper. All week I had done my part of the job with Timmy, sustaining the emotional distance I had established after the fight. Now I felt good. I was sure I had finally found the answer.

33

At dinner, however, I was surprised at how much time Carol and I spent discussing Timmy. Finally, I said, almost in exasperation, "Look, I put this great effort into this kid and he's only gotten worse! I'm just not going to do it anymore. That's it."

Carol stared at me. Quietly she said, "This sounds serious. And it's not a good situation for either of you. You know . . ." she got up and went over to the sideboard for more French bread, ". . . I met a psychologist at school last week who counsels teachers about problems in the classroom. Maybe I should give you his name."

"Do you really think so?" I asked as she sat back down. I wanted so to believe that things were now okay because I felt better, but somehow, I knew Carol was right.

"Well, how does he make you feel?"

I glanced around his small office, already feeling oppressed. Rolph was a large bearlike man with black curly hair and a large bushy black beard that had two lines of white running down it, almost like the tail on a skunk. I spent a great deal of time staring at it that first day in his too-small office. I felt that there was barely enough room—with his bulk and the immensity of my feelings—for me to breathe.

"Actually," I answered stiffly, clearing my throat, "I would like your guidance." Guidance, I thought, about what? Does this psychologist know what a basket case I am?

I had taken care this morning with my appearance. Earrings, a skirt and shoes, not my usual daycare attire. Today I wore them like a mask. Maybe if I dress right he won't know, I thought. *Know what?*

"Actually," I said, "I am here because I need your help." He rubbed his beard as he smiled at me encouragingly, his warm brown eyes catching a glint of the light. Need help? That sounds like I don't know what I am doing. Very unprofessional.

I leaned forward on my chair. "Not help exactly," I

quickly explained, "just guidance. Guidance about . . ." getting Timmy out of my house, my life, my thoughts. Looking up, I said gently, "about letting a child go."

"Oh, the child we discussed on the phone?" He adjusted his large, heavy frame in his chair.

"Yes, that one." I sat back in my chair and took a deep breath. "The child I called you about makes me feel like a hateful person, Rolph. I don't like using the gestapo tactics I have to use to control him. Last week I just gave up all the tender feelings I had for him. It felt better, for a while. But now his behavior has just gotten worse. It's hard for me because I think I hate him."

"Why the tears?" he asked gently, fingering his beard.

"Because children need love." And I couldn't stop crying. Well, here I go again—more tears for Timmy.

After I withdrew from him, Timmy simply got worse, and even though I was letting Barbara handle him and so felt better, every chance he got over the past week, he had grabbed at my face or my hands, still trying to get me to listen. If I didn't give him my full attention 100 percent of the time, he'd take it out on the other children, especially Jeffie.

Just prior to my calling Rolph, he had had a horrible cold, with green snot running from his nose all the time. I'd look at him and think, How can I love you? I absolutely hate your behavior, you're certainly not getting any better—in fact, you're getting worse.

"The reason why his behavior has accelerated," Rolph said to me, "is exactly because of your withdrawal. It is clear to me from what you've told me that Timmy feels secure with you."

I humphed as I wiped my nose. "I can't believe that. I'm just someone for him to pee on, poo on, bite, and kick. I don't think I can keep pretending I can handle it."

He wanted me to become Timmy D. and feel his feelings. At first I resisted this role playing. I didn't know how to do it and doubted that it would work. But by the second session, I suspended my disbelief and let myself become Timmy when he had those awful sores on his feet. As I put myself in his place, sitting in the kitchen sink, I could feel how powerless he was. His mother didn't understand what he needed but figured it was best for him to work it out for himself. His father thought he was giving him a gift by teaching him karate to make him stronger. And his brother responded to his aggressive signals with aggression. "Hey, Timmy!" I imagined him saying. "Want me to push you?"

"Yeah, push me *fast!*"

"Okay, you asked for it!"

I felt myself looking up helplessly out of that sink.

And I saw the moment when he and Jeffie were fighting and I told him that I didn't want him at my place anymore. I remembered how stunned he was as he handed Jeffie's pluggie back. He was terribly upset at what I had said because he wanted to be here. Barbara and I responded to him; even our dog Sandy listened to him!

And then I understood: he can't stop it because he doesn't know how. In that instant, I felt Timmy's anger and hopelessness. And I felt my love for him.

In the third session, Rolph began to give me the tool I was seeking. He said, "You're teaching Timmy how to speak. You can teach him how to moderate his aggression." He felt that Timmy needed a longer fuse. He didn't have a graduated sense of being annoyed, then irritated, then finally provoked to anger. A mistaken push and he would go straight to acting out rage.

"I know you're right," I said to him at the beginning of that session. "I've been thinking about this a lot. My whole philosophy of discipline is to give a child some alternative to inappropriate behavior. But when it comes to Timmy, I've just been too exhausted and too much in a state of crisis to think of philosophy, much less an alternative plan." I looked at Rolph. "Show me what I can do. I want to work with Timmy. I no longer want him to go away."

In that session, Rolph also helped me feel that it was okay to pick Timmy up, carry him away, and restrain him in his furies. He led me to see that I was not being an insensitive and cruel Nazi agent when I protected the children and myself from his assaults. And he guided me to see that what was needed now were words for his feelings. Words in place of action.

At the end of the session, I was even able to smile. "The truth is, there's a certain charm about Timmy D. I guess there must have been a certain charm about Al Capone too."

Driving home after that session, I thought about how he was such a tough little kid on the outside, but just as needy as Jeffie on the inside. They were both puddles of feelings. And when I allowed it, Timmy hit a soft spot in me. Every time I thought of him crying in the sink, his feet so raw and hurt, words of anger bubbling up for the first time: "I hate . . . John. He . . . hurts . . . me . . . all the time," I was moved. It was such an enormous gift for this child to finally have language. And now we were going to use it.

He needed us and wanted us—even after my explosion. We knew because originally he had only come mornings but after he pleaded, his mother was letting him come all day.

Still, I felt chilled at the thought of having to deal with his acting out for even one more day.

9

Lengthening a
Short Fuse

A LL RIGHT," I SAID. "I think I'm almost ready." Rolph had just said, "He trusted you to help him speak, he'll trust you with this too." He and I took our roles. Rolph became Timmy and I practiced what I would say to him.

A half hour later, I pulled my car into the driveway and walked through the back gate to the play yard where I found Barbara outside with all the children. I took Timmy out of the sandbox, led him by the hand to the deck, and sat him opposite me in one of the deck chairs. I took both sides of his helmeted face in mine and looked him right in the eyes the way he did me.

Then I said, "Timmy, this last month has been very hard for me. You're being irritable, you're being angry. I want you to know that's how I've been feeling too. When you hit and

38

holler and scream and yell, I want to do the same thing. I was really afraid that I would get angry with you and then I did. So I asked Barbara to take care of you. It made you madder and it made things worse. I understand now.

"And I want you to know, Timmy," I smiled at him for the first time in weeks, "you and I are going to deal with it. We're going to be friends. I have some things I am going to tell you when you're angry."

I didn't expect him to understand all these words but I knew I was communicating that I cared. How do I know? He hit me. Whenever he felt safe with me, he hit me. That much I had learned.

So from then on for every situation, I taught him to describe his anger. We used four words: I'm *annoyed*. I'm *irritated*. I'm *mad*. I'm *angry*.

Every day I watched him very carefully for any signs of anger. "Timmy," I stopped him. "You're irritated because Jeffie knocked over your building. He didn't mean to. This is no big deal. This is called 'being irritated.'"

He said, "t-t-tated."

"That's right. When you're irritated what you say is, 'Don't knock over my building.' Say that to Jeffie." And he said that to Jeffie, and Jeffie said, "I didn't mean to." Then I said, "It was an accident, Timmy. Everybody has accidents. It's all right now, just build your building." He would.

If someone hit him, I was right there. "Oh, you're mad. Tell Doug that you're mad at him and not to hit you."

"I'm mad. Don't hit, or I'm gonna—" and I said, "You don't have to say that part. All you have to tell him is not to do that to you. You don't have to threaten him."

One day, I said, "You're mad."

He looked at me, "No, I angry."

I laughed and said to him, "What you do when you're angry is you shout." And he shouted, "I'm angry!"

"What you do when you're angry is you stamp your

feet!'' And he shouted and stamped his feet. "Say, 'I'm angry! I'm angry!' and stamp your feet.'' And he did. Along with every other child in the playroom who was listening in.

Rolph suggested that we buy a punching bag for Timmy to beat up. So the next time he was in a black mood I brought out Bozo, one of those inflatable knockdown, bounce-back toys.

Timmy punched it and it bounced back and hit him. He hit it again and it bounced back and hit him. "K. Now I mad.''

He hit it and it bounced back and hit him again. He stamped his feet, threw himself on it, and bit it.

He ran out to me in the yard and said, "I kill Bozo.''

I followed him back to the playroom. Bozo lay very flat on the floor. We had Bozo with us for all of twenty minutes.

Next, Rolph suggested a punching bag. So I got the kind that hung down from a stand. Well, Timmy stood on the stand and hit it with such force that it came back and hit him square in the face and knocked him down.

He wanted to kill it. "Where is it?'' he said. "I'm gonna—''

I got rid of it by putting it down in our basement. I told Rolph at our next session about it.

"This is getting ridiculous,'' I said.

"How about pillows?'' he said.

10

Joanie!
Be a Traffic Light!

J OANIE, WILL YOU BE the traffic light for our road?"
I was sitting out in the play yard observing the
children when Bobby asked me.

"You already have a traffic light," I said. "Teresa."

"We need two traffic lights. One for here and one for
over there."

Jennifer and Bobby were riding in cars and wanted to
be stopped or let go at two points as they traveled the rect-
angle of cement work that was their road around the bark
box.

"Can't you get someone else to be a traffic light?" I
asked hopefully.

"No one else wants to play."

I knew that, but gave it a try anyway because I hate to
be a traffic light.

"Okay, I'll play—for a little while."

41

They only heard the okay. They were off to their cars. Teresa was sitting on the bench directly across the bark box from me. She had both hands up which looked like go. When Jen and Bobby came around she put both arms out. It looked like stop to me. Bobby and Jennifer stopped. They waited. Teresa continued the stop sign. Then she raised her arms and said, "Go." They went. Then they looked across the bark box at me. I already had my arms up for go just as I had seen Teresa do it.

They came around and I put my arms down and said, "Stop."

They said, "You don't *say* stop. You just do that with your arms and we will stop."

I said, "Teresa said, 'Go' when she put her arms up. Why can't I say 'Stop' when I put my arms down?"

Jennifer tossed her curls. "'Cause you can't."

"Oh," I said.

I put my arms up for Go and they went. I rested my elbows on the arms of my chair, continuing to keep my forearms and hands up. I was watching Jeffie play by himself across the yard when I realized they were coming toward me again.

They called to me, "*Joanie!* Be a traffic light."

I said, "I *am,* I am ready for you." Something about the way Jeffie was playing bothered me.

I put my arms out for Stop as they came to me. They stopped. I was noticing that when other children went up to Jeffie to talk or play, he turned from them or sent them away. That was very odd. Jeffie always liked to play with other children.

I put my arms up and said, "Go."

Bobby leaned over his car door and said, "You don't have to say, 'Go.' You're a traffic light—you can't talk."

I said, "Oh."

Around they went again. The thing that was odd about Jeffie's play was that it was so low-key and quiet. This was not like him. I had no idea what he was doing over there.

Jennifer and Bobby appeared before me before I was aware of their approach. I quickly put my arms out for Stop. They stopped. I put my arms up for Go. They went. I called across the yard to Jeff. He looked up at me, furtively got up, and went into the house.

Bobby called across the yard, "*Joanie!* Be a traffic light!"

I said, "I am," quickly putting my arms up.

"No, you weren't."

I said, "Look at Teresa—she's climbing on the tree—you're not hollering at her!"

Jennifer called to her, "Teresa, are you playing?"

"Yes," Teresa said from the tree which was near her spot.

Jennifer turned to me and said, "See, she's playing."

Yes, she was. The truth was Teresa *is* a traffic light. I am not. And Bobby and Jennifer know this. I cannot be a traffic light no matter how hard I concentrate on being one because I am only pretending. Teresa, however, is a traffic light, so she gets to climb trees.

I found Jeffie in the back of the small playroom, alone by the window. I sat down on the sofa and watched.

Ostensibly, he was playing by himself with a small green truck in the corner. The only trouble was that he was not playing like the rambunctious little noise box that I knew. I sat there and thought about the last few months and the curious change in him.

Jeffie had been growing steadily happier and more confident. When he came to us he was a very needy child. His parents were separating and it was tough. Jeffie cried so much and I was spending so much time holding him that I hired my son Tim to take my place in the rocking chair. Over time, Jeff became less needy and more vocal—not verbally necessarily, but he always had a sound for everything he noticed. And he noticed everything!

His hair was cut in the shape of a bowl and he had

Groucho Marx–like eyebrows, very expressive. Perhaps I looked to them so much and his sparkling eyes because he always had his pacifier in his mouth. In fact, he always had two pacifiers with him, one in his mouth and the other, his sniffing pluggie, he held to his nose. It was very old, smelly, and rather grotesque and he loved it dearly. At one point, early in his first few months, Barbara and I took a string and put a row of five pluggies on it to let him know that he didn't have to worry so much about misplacing one. He wore it like a necklace around his neck. Now there were enough pluggies in the world.

As Jeffie settled in, he exhibited a radiant sense of humor. His eyes danced, his cheeks flushed, and he laughed so ecstatically that I always joined in. It was fun to be around him.

He had trouble pronouncing the letter *l*. Whenever he tried his pluggie would shoot out of his mouth and everyone would laugh. It hurt his feelings. Finally one day I said, "Jeffie, what if every time I said the letter *s* my hair flew off?" He looked at me and his eyes danced. His eyebrows shot up and he laughed.

He was unusually perceptive for a three-year-old. He would take four horses and make a sculpture out of them, and at the end, turn one upside down and laugh and laugh. He loved to do something perfectly and then leave one part awry so he could giggle at it.

I wear Birkenstock sandals. One day I was out in the yard fixing a tire on one of our tricycles. I was concentrating very hard when Jeffie started to laugh. I looked up at him and he pointed to my foot. In my concentration I had lifted my big toe up in an odd angle and he thought that was just hysterical.

What a lovable little boy, I thought as I watched him play. He loved me too. One day he crawled up on my lap, stroked my face, and called me Joanie. He was the first to call me that since my father. Now all the children and most of the parents call me Joanie. And he was the one who named me.

So much had happened these last few months, I thought. Maybe that's why he's withdrawn a bit. When he first came to us he ate two-fistedly and with such gusto that food often got caught in his hair. Once when I was reading to the children, a piece of corn popped out of Jeffie's ear! Now he had taught himself how to use a fork and was eating more calmly.

He was acting very grown-up lately. In fact, he was becoming almost philosophical about things. Recently, when Timmy once again pounced on him, taking one of his pluggies, Jeffie let him walk away with it. "There are plenty of pluggies for me," he said.

I told his mother, Nancy, and we were both pleased about it. He ate with a fork, he didn't let Timmy upset him as much, and a few days ago, the pluggie necklace we had given him ended up around Sandy's neck after school. It seemed that Jeffie didn't need it anymore.

The next day, I got down on the floor and sat near him as he played alone. "Jeffie," I said quietly, "what are you doing?"

He looked up at me, startled.

"Did I frighten you?"

"No," he said.

"What are you playing?" I asked.

He looked at me and his thick eyebrows shot up. "Well, Joanie," he said, "it's dangerous."

11

Playing Baby

HEN A MIRACLE HAPPENED WITH TIMMY. They say that miracles surround us all the time if we can but see them. I began to see one: Timmy D. began using words more than he did his fists.

First of all, he actually developed a sense of humor about himself. He'd pretend he was going to hit someone and make the jerk, and I'd react like I had for so many months and be right there, and he'd look at me and laugh. "I only annoyed. Don't worry."

Secondly, he began to listen to the books I read. He finally was able to settle down enough that he had room for us and for the other children. Because he was not acting out all the time, he could identify with the good guys and enjoy the action in a story.

And he began to play baby.

We have a very large cradle for dolls that is strong enough for children to fit into. Timmy D. started playing

46

family with two friends. I became fascinated with how they would play.

Bart's dad was always saying to him, "Bart, you have to be Number 1. You have to be Number 1 in everything you do. If you're not Number 1, it's not worth doing."

Diane's parents, on the other hand, were separating at this time, and she was very lonely, not only because of the divorce, but because she had a brand-new baby sister. And, then, of course, there was Timmy D., our angry young boy.

These were the difficulties in their lives that each brought to their play to work out. And they played each part—mother, father, baby—continually changing roles, for months. In those early years of my daycare, I was beginning to realize that children make sense of their reality by playing out what's on their minds.

Each one was in the cradle for days at a time. When Bart was the baby, he'd just lay there. He didn't cry or laugh or ask for anything. So mommy and daddy, Diane and Timmy, had to always ask what he wanted. Or they'd guess at it.

"Oh," they'd say, "you're hungry." And together they'd give him the bottle.

"Oh," they'd say, "you want to be rocked?"

Diane, on the other hand, asked for everything all the time, crying and laughing and gurgling and speaking baby talk. And Bart and Timmy gave her everything they could.

But Timmy. He would cry the entire time he was in the cradle. It would go on for an hour. Diane and Bart would rock and rock him. They would take off his football helmet and stroke his hair and kiss him. Timmy would just lie there and cry and cry, and they would wipe away each pretend tear.

Then it would be someone else's turn. They always knew when the right time was. They never fought over whose turn it was which I felt was amazing, particularly because of Timmy's behavior up until this point. I was beginning to realize how powerful the play that the children structured for themselves was. Consequently, it felt less necessary to offer them specific times for crayons, paint at the easel, Play-Doh at the table—*my* structure for the day. Left to themselves, these children seemed to be forming their own community.

Timmy would get out of the cradle and Bart would crawl in. And Diane and Timmy would do the same thing for him. "Oh, you want your hair brushed?" And they would do it. There was definitely something in it for each child for they continued it every day for many weeks.

Around this time, I asked a friend of mine, Thayer Jones, who I had worked with in the Berkeley Public Schools before opening my own daycare, to make a film. I thought it would be fun for the children and interesting for the parents to see. In the film, Hildegard, our music teacher, is playing the accordion and the children surround her singing; some are dancing. In the film it becomes evident as we watch that Timmy and Diane want desperately to be with her but there's baby Bart in the cradle and they are on the other side of the room. They can't just leave their baby. They look toward the music and then back at baby and then toward the music again. I remember being tempted to help them and then thinking better of it. Perhaps they would discover their own way. Finally, they get together and pull the cradle all the way over to the other side of the playroom. Now they can sing as well as tend baby.

I was always moved as I watched them. It was all gentleness this play, nothing but gentleness.

But, nevertheless, we had a lot of work to do. Timmy's outbursts were much less but they still were very much there.

12

Crisis over Timmy

Y OU'RE GOING TO WHAT?" I said, my knees beginning
to tremble. We were standing on the front deck
right by the lemon tree. I put my hand on the tree
to steady myself.

"We're going to take Timmy out. He's four
now and so socially developed that Anthony and I feel he's
ready for an academic program. At Country School he'll
learn—"

My head started to spin. But we're not through yet! I cried
out to myself. There's so much more he needs to do, to experience. Let's not leave this unfinished. Please, let this go on.

But I didn't say a word to her.

"Why not?" Carol Washburn asked. We were sitting at
the kitchen table having a cup of coffee.

49

"Because she doesn't listen to a word I say." I fiddled with my cup.

"You know what, Joan? You didn't do your work," Carol said gently. "It takes a while to become a real pro at this, and you have to want to do it. Like it or not, children bring their families to daycare. And it's essential that you talk to their parents, sharing your feelings with them and letting them share with you. All the time."

"I do! But Jackie won't listen."

"Look what Tina gets—" and she glanced over at her daughter, happily playing near us. "Because you and I sit and talk to each other. And you do that with Bart's mother too and Diane's dad so they get to know you and trust your judgment."

"But Jackie and Anthony won't let me tell them a thing."

"But they want to know what you know about Timmy. You need to find a way to let them in. You need them, too, Joan—their feelings and insights are great resources that you can draw upon."

She thought for a moment. "They've no idea what you've gone through with him, do they?" she asked quietly.

"They won't let me—every time I get near either of them I feel a barrier. They don't want to hear the bad stuff."

"Joan," she said, "I know how hard it is for you to communicate with Timmy's parents, but try to put yourself in their shoes." She stood up. "How would you feel if someone had an intimate two-year relationship with your child in which that person struggled to help him to become well adjusted and you don't even know how that happened?" She sat down with the coffeepot and leaned toward me. She was a beautiful woman, very smart and vibrant and caring. "And not only that, but that person who worked with your child had shared this experience with others. So that other people were walking around knowing intimate things that you haven't been told about!" She looked at me squarely. "That feels pretty yucky to me. Don't you think you've made some judgments about Timmy's parents and that's the barrier to including them?"

And I started to cry. Because she was so right.

13

The Conference

BARBARA," I SAID TO HER as we shampooed the carpets one Saturday. "How does this sound . . . ?" I was practicing for the conference I was going to have with Anthony and Jackie. " 'Timmy has his friends here, children who've learned to know and love him. Just like you saw in the film where he played baby, our daycare is a place where Timmy can continue to grow and be loved.' Then I'll remind them that this is where he wants to be. When Timmy started, he came only mornings and then wanted to be here in the afternoons too, five days a week. I'll remind them how Timmy has learned to talk, to express his anger appropriately, and he has a sense of humor now which I think is enchanting."

"*Enchanting?*" Barbara sniffed. "Isn't that laying it on a bit thick?"

I practiced by myself up in my sunny room overlooking the play yard. It was so important that I got it right. "I'll ask them about Country School to see what appeals to them, why they like it and see Timmy in it. If it's just academics, I'll point out that you don't send your four-year-old to a school— you send them to a person." I gazed at the plum tree beneath the window and thought, if I hadn't been withdrawn from them they would know these things already. "Then, of course I'll get down to it," I said, continuing to practice aloud. "I'll have to tell them about my own feelings and fears. I'll begin, 'I don't think I've really said much to you two about the personal relationship between Timmy and me . . .' "

The day before the conference I also practiced with Carol and then ended by saying, "I'm so nervous. How will I be able to say, 'This is what I have been doing the last two years with your child'? It feels like I intentionally kept secrets. How are they going to feel about me?"

Yet I was resolved to do it. It was the only hope I had of their reconsidering letting Timmy spend one more year with us.

"Tell them you're nervous," Carol said.

"Really?"

"Yes, she's a therapist and you're nervous about it. So begin with that."

"I'm very nervous about this," I said, smiling at them. It was a Friday evening and we were in the big playroom. I had made a large roaring fire and was seated in a comfortable chair across from them. They were on the sofa directly facing the fire and me, and all our toys now brightly stacked away on the shelves. "You're a therapist, Jackie, and it makes me feel a little insecure. But I would like to share with the both of you a little bit about Timmy's life at our daycare and how I see his progress—"

"Well, we're kind of nervous too," Anthony said. "Because we have a baby-sitter and only have about twenty minutes here before we have to be at our movie."

That was how it began.

I pushed on. I told them about how Timmy and I had spent a lot of time working on what to do when you're angry. "Oh, yes," Jackie interrupted. "He's so well adjusted. It's great. That's what's made us feel he should go to Country School and have a bit of an academic experience to prepare him for kindergarten."

"Yes, Timmy is a wonderful little boy and has learned a lot—" I said. Anthony was gazing at his watch. "—but I don't think he is ready for academic experiences just yet."

"Oh, well," Jackie said, "we feel—" and she talked for the next ten minutes about the importance of a more structured prekindergarten experience.

When she finally stopped, I asked them how they felt about all the changes in Timmy. Their response was they didn't feel that he was hitting as much as he used to.

I continued on course. "You saw the film when we had all the parents here—what were your feelings when you saw Timmy in it?" At this point a conflict arose, because Jackie liked it and Anthony didn't. They started to argue about the value of regression. Anthony wanted him to stop playing baby and "get back to growing up." Jackie didn't think Anthony should be teaching Timmy karate anymore. She liked the budding tenderness she observed in him. This took up our last five minutes.

Anthony glanced at his watch. "Well, Joan . . ." and he stood up. They had already made up their minds.

But still I quickly said, "It's very important that Timmy stay here so that he continues to have experiences to reinforce the behavior that you value. It's so new and untested with him that I truly believe that he would benefit from the additional year here."

Anthony said, "Thank you very much."

"We'll let you know," Jackie said as she stood up.

That was it. I didn't get a chance to go into anything else—the therapy, the tantrums—nothing. The next week they took him out and I never saw Timmy D. again.

14

In Search of Jeffie

A FEW DAYS AFTER TIMMY LEFT, I joined Jeffie, once such a little boy of excess, as he played with one tiny car in his spot in the playroom. I felt very confused about him and myself as I sat near him. Here was a little boy who had taken up so much room—at one point he collected all the green things in the playroom and surrounded himself with them. The other children all assumed that they were his, from "his house," and would ask his permission to use anything green. He perpetually carried around his pluggies, his beloved blanket, and a huge green airplane. Now he was alone, without green, only one pluggie, and no collection of toys. And I felt very inadequate as I sat there.

I was sick to death of all the surprises I had been through lately. Timmy's leaving was not the only upset, by any means. Just a few months earlier Emily's parents unexpectedly transferred her to a French day school so she could begin learning a second language. And just three weeks ago, I found out—two months after the fact from her mother—that the reason Teresa had been so unhappy was because her parents had separated.

Maybe Carol is right, I thought, as I watched Jeffie turn his little car over and over again. She is always saying to me that children bring their families to daycare. This was a depressing thought, for I hadn't figured out what I was supposed to do with them.

And now, what do I do about Jeffie? Where is this little boy? I had asked Rolph, "Where is he all day? He used to be a little noise box with an opinion about everything, and now he's so quiet."

"I don't know the answers to any of that," he said. "But Jeffie does. If you want to know where he spends his time, ask him."

So here I was, sitting near him in the playroom. I asked, "What are you thinking about?"

Jeffie looked up at me. His thick eyebrows shot up in the old way, but he said, "Please go away."

"Can't I sit here?" I asked in amazement.

"No," he said and picked up his car defensively.

I continued to observe his play from a distance. I felt so incompetent. Rolph helped me to face this uncomfortable feeling, letting me see how ridiculous it was. Here I was, being congratulated all the time by parents for my work! All had seen other daycares and could see the difference. Children were treated here with respect and love. They eagerly looked forward to coming. When they came home at night they were happier and more independent of their parents. They slept better with fewer nightmares. Above all, each one seemed to be developing a level of competence and self-esteem that was truly remarkable.

Yet, as I sat on the sofa watching Jeffie, I was at sea. He had made great strides toward independence these past few months; he needed only one pluggie now, he ate with a fork, he had stood up for himself with Timmy, and, until very recently, he had many friends. But with Rolph's guidance I was realizing that there was a whole area of this child I didn't know. Perhaps he has needs he can't ask for. But how can we find out what they are?

"You're going to have to get down there and play what he's playing."

"I can't. He won't let me." I was back in Rolph's office.

"Joan, you know this is serious. Whenever there is suddenly a significant change in a child's behavior it is very important to find out why."

"Yes, I know that. But—Rolph. It doesn't feel right." I leaned forward in my chair. "You're always asking me about my feelings. Well, I don't feel right about playing with my kids. I talk to them. I share with them. I observe them. But the play is theirs."

"Then tell me how you are going to find out where he is if you don't join him there."

I told him about the traffic light incident. "I am a terrible traffic light but Teresa *is* a traffic light. Adults aren't good at playing with three-year-olds. If they were they'd be demented."

Rolph laughed.

I continued, "I've learned to let children work things out for themselves, like Jennifer wanting so badly to live with me and playing it out with her dolly, or Timmy D., playing baby. You know, the day he left," I smiled, "he was playing baby with my dog Sandy. He covered her with a blanket, told her to stay, and combed her fur and sang to her. This little boy knows how to take care of himself now. When Jackie came to get him, he ran over to Sandy and stared in her eyes and petted her good-bye."

"All right," Rolph said, bringing me back to here and now. "But how are you going to do for Jeffie what you've done for Timmy?"

That was the question. As I drove home, I thought to myself that I really didn't know the answer. Jeffie had withdrawn, and once again I didn't seem to have the tools to bring him back. Rolph was the professional, so I thought, I have to go along with him. But something still bothered me.

The next day, I went back to Jeffie's spot in the small playroom where he stayed most of the time. I tried to put myself in his place and feel what he was feeling. I felt scared.

I waited for a while, just watching him turn the single block in his hand over and over again.

"Jeffie?" I said, finally.

He looked up.

I swallowed. "Can I play with you?"

He looked down at his block. "It's dangerous. I told you that." And then he looked up and smiled.

15

Why Am I Doing Daycare?

NO, SANDY, THERE ARE NO CHILDREN TODAY. It's Saturday." The plump dog wagged her tail. She had been waiting since early morning for the children to arrive. She did this every Saturday. Then, as if she finally understood, she lumbered slowly back up the stairs and, filled with disappointment, plopped herself down on the landing and stuck her head out over it, watching me down below.

I was waiting for Carol Washburn to arrive to help me plant new flowers on the deck. I love my house. It seems to appreciate in value at about the same level as I need money. And I enjoy keeping it up.

I didn't know how bad I felt until Carol and I were on our knees weeding the huge barrels filled with flowers out front.

"I keep asking myself lately, why am I doing daycare? It isn't the money. I could make more money working for the telephone company. First Timmy D., then little Jeffie, who was such an outgoing boy and suddenly has become so withdrawn." I looked at her. "Recently I asked him what he was playing and he told me it was dangerous. *This worries me.* And now I've lost confidence because of yesterday! How can I work with other parents' children when one of mine is in trouble?"

"Joan." Carol put down her trowel. "Just because your fifteen-year-old got drunk doesn't mean she's in trouble and you're a failure!"

"But she was passed out cold on our front yard just as parents were picking up their children at five-thirty on a Friday afternoon—"

Carol wouldn't stop laughing. "Nobody expects you to be perfect. Things happen."

Actually it was sort of amusing if you weren't her mother. Barbara and I quickly carried her inside and put her on the sofa in the playroom and redirected all the traffic into the hallway and other rooms. When Dr. Washburn came—Tina's father—we scooted him in to see Karen. He doesn't carry a doctor's bag so he borrowed one of the toy stethoscopes to examine her, one he has borrowed before since we impose upon him often. He pronounced her fine—just drunk.

I sighed. "I've been thinking a lot about what you've said, Carol. I know you were right about Anthony and Jackie. I was thinking about that time I went outside to talk to him after he dropped Timmy off so abruptly. I know why he drove away. He felt just like I do when one of my children's teachers needs to speak to me about something they've done. I get defensive too, don't want to hear, and want to drive off. I bet those were his feelings." I looked at her. "There must be a way for me to include parents in all of this instead of pushing them away."

"Oh, yes!" she said as she vigorously pushed her trowel hard in the soil. "Parents want to hear what you have to say. We need you. It's more difficult with some parents for sure, probably the ones who need you most." She smiled encouragingly. "Just as you call Elizabeth, Karen's high school teacher, when you've needed to talk about Karen, I really need you with Tina. I don't have any distance; as a mother, I don't think I'm supposed to."

I went back to my weeding and I thought about Karen and how grateful I was that Elizabeth was her teacher and friend and that she understood and respected parents. When I called her last night immediately after the parents had all left, she reminded me that children learn by experience and that I should feel grateful that Karen, instead of hiding out, could come home where she was safe. This was a tribute to my mothering. Then I thought about Jeffie and how he didn't seem to need us anymore. I didn't know what to do—to let him just work it out himself or try to help him.

After a few moments, I said aloud, "I believe in *permission*."

"Yes?" Carol looked over at me. She was used to this. We often started in the middle of a thought with each other.

I sat back on my heels. "You know, when I was a child, I would come running to my parents all filthy from playing, my dress in tatters—" I laughed. "I was a very dirty little girl, I never liked to have my hair brushed and braided. I was too busy! And my father, who was truly an intellectual, would be there having his discussions with his friends and he always welcomed me. They loved to have me around. And no matter how awful I behaved they just loved me anyway. You have to have a lot of confidence in yourself to let your children be themselves and not feel that what they do reflects on you. If a teacher criticized me, they thought he or she was just blind not to see how wonderful I was. Their message to me was, 'My, aren't you doing well!' I knew when I was doing badly so what I needed to hear—and, of course, can we ever hear it enough?—'My, aren't you doing wonderfully.' So I grew up thinking I could do anything. It may take time, I may feel discouraged, but by my own efforts, I will succeed."

I got up off my heels. "I'm just developing this idea, Carol, but I think there's a method in dealing with children that has to do with respecting them and having faith that somehow or other they know what they're doing. And very often, if left alone, they do it right for themselves. Like Timmy." I brushed off my pants. "I intervened in his tantrums because he was hurting others. But I would not intervene in play that a child was doing to work out something." I smiled at her. "You and I talk and talk. And children play and play."

I opened the front door for her and stopped. "I think that's probably what will turn out to be the most valuable thing that really goes on in this place." I followed her out of the bright sun into the cool darkness of our hallway. "What it seems to be about is having faith that a child is going to do what he needs to do to become the best he can be. Our job is to support him in his efforts. This is what I got from my parents."

"Well, I guess the question is," Carol said as she opened the package of coffee in the kitchen, "do you think Jeffie is going to make it? Without your intervening?"

After Carol left, I went upstairs to my room. Sandy followed and arranged herself by the wood-burning stove. Karen was still resting in her room. My thirteen-year-old, Laura, was spending the night at a friend's. And my two sons, Tim and John, were away at college. My husband George had moved out a few years before. We had been childhood sweethearts in St. Louis since he was thirteen and I was twelve. When we split I hurt so much my teeth ached. Still, it was the right thing to do.

Across from me, behind the stove, was a picture of my father sitting in a boat fishing on a great lake. In this picture he seems very small and the lake very large.

If I don't do this work, I thought as I gazed at that very large lake, what will I do? I chose to do this work out of the vision I had begun to develop when I worked with my teacher friend, Thayer, in his fourth-, fifth-, and sixth-grade combination class in the Berkeley Public Schools. Prior to that time, raising my four children was all that I did. Then when my son Tim was enrolled in Thayer's experimental class, I threw myself into working in the classroom. I taught students, raised money, talked to the school board, and helped evaluate our experimental classroom. Then in the early seventies the money ran out, the mood changed, and my children were out of grammar school. I was left with this magnificent experience. I had seen children by their own efforts manage their own lives and make appropriate choices. Much of what we did in Thayer's class was designed to give children power. With our support, they had the freedom to choose to study or do what interested them. They learned to read, write, and do math; children who had been truly deficient in all areas came away knowing that they could learn and choose well for themselves. I wanted to continue this work but I didn't want to do it in a school system.

And I remembered the wonderful experience I had had years before when I put myself through college by working at Mother Hubbard's Dingdong Daycare in Wichita, Kansas. I still laugh to myself when I remember that name. And I remember thinking when the experimental class was over, what if I tried this with three- and four-year-olds—supported them in their efforts to manage their own lives? What if I let them decide how they will spend their day, what they will eat, and let them choose their own activities? I believed that I could support them in creating their own place, a community of children who would learn what they needed to know to belong. And if I started my own daycare, in my own home, I would have real control over it. And that is exactly what I did.

Now I live, eat, breathe daycare. When the work is going well, there is nothing like the high I feel when a child has a dilemma and solves it. That's how I felt with Jennifer. She had a problem and worked on it, by trial and error, until she solved it.

Why do I care so much? I thought of my father and the passion he had for his work. The photo of him fishing was taken the summer after he lost his job as a social worker because he fought against anti-Semitism just after the war. A Jewish man he fought alongside of gave him the money, after he was fired, to buy a fishing resort. "Go fish, Phil," he said. "Time heals all wounds."

But for my father it didn't. And though he loved me to death, my childhood ended when I was eleven, the year my brother died and my father lost his job and we stopped celebrating Christmas.

And I sat there in my old soft chair and realized that the reason I do what I do started long before, when I began the fight to have Christmas for another child.

16

Do You See the Green Light?

I NEVER FOR ONE MOMENT had to do anything to win my father's heart. When I was eleven, we did what was important together. Mother stayed home with my younger brother where she liked to be. Dad and I were out—in the yard, in the car, on the boat. We fished. We planned and dreamed on winter evenings while we rolled Sir Walter Raleigh tobacco into cigarettes, each one rolled the same as each of the others, tightly and uniformly into neat stacks of twenty, while we planned our summer vacation. We tied the flies that caught our large-mouthed bass in June and we organized the tackle box while we planned. As soon as vacation was over we planned the Fourth of July. Picnic! Fireworks! On the boat? At the shore? After that, we planned Labor Day, last fishing for the season, and talked of ice fishing at Thanksgiving.

"But let's not get ahead of ourselves," Dad would say because our enthusiasm always carried us forward. "One thing at a time, Joanie. Stay on course." The biggest temptation of all being, of course, to shoot straight for Christmas.

We got through Thanksgiving—big dinner, festivities with others, and ice fishing all the long weekend. But what was most notable for me was that it passed. Because on the Friday after Thanksgiving we could begin.

We followed our plan. Step one was breakfast, step two was usually ice fishing. And step three was getting properly settled there—such delicious agony all this stifling of ourselves! Then we could finally begin.

We each wanted the other to go first.

"You first."

"No, you."

"No, you're first."

"No."

"Okay."

Dad knew when I really wanted him to go first.

"Last year," he began as he baited his hook, "although it was a beautiful tree—I'm not saying it wasn't, Joanie—it did, however, lean a bit toward the left."

"Yes, I noticed that too." I handed him a weight. "Just at the very top," I said.

"But beautiful," he said.

It was difficult for us to make disparaging remarks about last year's tree because we were sure each Christmas that we had found the perfect one. So all this was a difficult but necessary process, for what we were planning was the perfect Christmas, and, perfection, as you know, when once achieved is by its very concept finished. And we weren't about to be finished with Christmas.

So for us, the perfect Christmas began with the perfect tree. This took many evenings after work and school, searching each lot until we found a number of trees in our category, a category established, by the way, that Friday after Thanksgiving as we ice fished. It would be a blue spruce, six to six and a half feet tall, and its bottom branches must be at least five feet wide.

It was decorated, as always, a week before Christmas. Afterward, we would lie under it, on our backs, our heads at exactly the middle, alongside of the trunk. Dad would be on one side and I on the other, our faces and hearts open to the lights and colors shining on the balls, the icicles shimmering, and all the ornaments vaguely moving above and around us. We lay quietly, becoming a part of the magic we had imagined and then made real.

We stayed still and silent for a while and then Dad would say, "Do you see the green light, the one just nearest to the yellow one, about midway up?"

I would strain to find the first green light—there were several in that direction—and then locate the one nearest a yellow.

"Got it."

"Now," he said. "Just to the left and above the yellow light? Do you see almost a rainbow of light on the crystal icicle—?"

"Yes—"

"—just to the left and a bit above the yellow light?"

"Yes."

"Do you see it?"

"Yes, I do see it! I do."

And as we lay there under the tree, we would start planning for Christmas Day. The shopping. Gifts for Mother. Stockings hung, candy for the tree, candy for the candy dishes, candy for me! A present for my teacher, presents for all of our friends. Our task was a delicious stream of detail and delight. Logs for the fire, wrapping paper, ribbon, wreaths, holly, garlands; our heads, as we lay under our perfect tree, were filled with Christmas smells and all that sparkled, shimmered, shone.

Then my younger brother died. Sandy had been ill with rheumatic fever as a very little boy. Then when he was five and I was eleven we both had our tonsils out. Same operation, same room. But he died in the night.

I remember running down the hall to get a nurse. The hall was filled with yellow light and it seemed such a very long one. At the end of it was the nurse's station where three nurses were talking to each other. They didn't notice me coming toward them. I had stopped running and was holding onto the wall because I felt dizzy. I couldn't talk because of the operation so I couldn't call to them. I got almost all the way to them before a nurse saw me and came toward me. She turned me around and lectured me all the way back to the room. "You shouldn't be out of bed," she said. "Look, you're barefoot."

I couldn't get her attention. I couldn't tell her. I remember it was the most horrible feeling. She was going to see this terrible thing that had happened in this room and her seeing it would make it real. Oh, I hoped it wasn't real.

We got in the room and she saw him. She ran out and hollered up the hall. All these nurses came running and suddenly there were gurneys and oxygen tanks and a screen between our two beds as they tried to revive him. Then they wheeled me away and put me in another room.

I came home in the morning. Relatives began to arrive and they had to tell me something. I kept wanting to know what was going on. They said that they just had to keep Sandy in the hospital a little longer.

I knew he was dead, though. I saw him half kneel in his crib and then fall. I heard him make that sound and turn that awful color.

But I didn't tell them that. I wanted it left unsaid too.

The next day I was sitting on the floor trying to make a bracelet of the meat rationing stamps that were left over from our trips to the butcher shop after the war.

Dad sat down next to me. He took the little disks from me and took my hands in his. "Sandy died, Joanie," he said. His eyes were almost pure liquid. "It wasn't the operation, it was his heart. He died because his heart was damaged." He cried deep sobs as we held each other. I cried too, for Sandy, for him and that he hurt so much, that he looked like that.

Two days later, my father was fired from his job. He had fought and lost his battle against prejudice at work, and a fraction of that loss was his job.

Our first Christmas after Sandy's death Dad said, "Mother

and I can't face Christmas this year." So we flew to Chicago and spent it with relatives, following their plans, their secrets. They did the best they could, but it was their Christmas, not ours.

Then, the fourth Christmas after Sandy's death, Mother was pregnant. When she told me, my first thought was, now we'll have to have Christmas.

I was met with a flood of tears. Dad once remarked, "Mother cries at menus." It was true, Mother leaked all over the place.

"It isn't your fault, Joan, it's just that I can't imagine Christmas without Sandy."

"Well, I can't imagine a baby without Christmas."

"I hadn't thought about that," she said as she wiped her eyes. "I suppose when it's older we'll have to."

"I want to have Christmas this year, Mother. Do it for me."

There. It was said.

She started to cry again, now full of guilt for not providing for one child because she couldn't for the other. But the next day she brought it up again. "Even if I could, I don't think Dad could. Do you know what I mean?"

"If he agrees, will you agree?" Sixteen, but ever the child.

"I don't think it's time yet. I don't think you should."

"I'm going to ask him. Please, please can I tell him you'll do it if he will?"

She paused. I knew I had won. She said, "Yes."

There was a strength in Mother and a depth that was not in Dad. She was more easily satisfied, less extravagant, more practical, better able to appreciate life as it unfolded. Dad was impatient. He made things happen.

She brought this strength to bear on my behalf for now we were both working on making Christmas happen this year. She wrote to Dad who was away for a few months trying to sell the resort.

"We'll see," he replied.

I wrote to Dad.

"We'll talk when I get back from the fishing resort. I miss you," he replied.

Finally, Dad had been home a week. Barbara was born; now there were four of us again. I brought it up.

"Labor Day is coming," I began.

He looked at me.

"I was just thinking how we used to take every special day, and, well, make it our own."

His face softened. "Yes, I guess so," he said.

"Help me, Dad. You know what I'm getting at."

"Yeh, I know." He was quiet. I was going to start up again when he said, "It seems what you have in mind is doing what we used to do at Christmas."

"Yes!"

"You're almost grown-up now. I mean, you're not a child. And I've changed too. Things are a bit different, don't you think?" His eyes smiled like they used to right before his mouth smiled and lit up his whole face.

"I want to have Christmas this year, Dad, with a tree, holly, a wreath on the front door, and presents. I want everything to sparkle and shimmer all over the house."

His eyes filled with pain. His mouth began to tremble. "Oh, God," he said, "I am so tired of crying." He tried to compose himself. "Christmas makes me cry, Joanie. I can't help it."

His sadness overwhelmed me. His tears, unlike Mother's, upset me terribly. I was just about to give up. But there was Mother. She sat down next to him and took his hand. He cried, but she didn't. I couldn't believe it. She didn't even look like she wanted to cry.

"Phil," she said. "We need to talk about this. We have Barbara now. And Joanie wants to. We need to have Christmas."

The next year, Mother and I planned Christmas. Over the months, we had grown close. I found I could excite her with my imagination, and she, me, with stories of her childhood. Together we bought a huge tree and put many lights on it. We spent all of one evening just placing the icicles, the way they should be hung on the branches, one by one by one. It was magnificent.

And we had Barbara, now seventeen months, beside herself with excitement. She hardly slept once in bed, so we often lay down beside her in Mother's big bed and continued our talk of what was to come: Santa, toys, candy, surprises, presents, stockings. We couldn't help ourselves; Barbara loved it all, and Mother and I, like her, were full of anticipation.

Dad came home Friday night as usual. It was Christmas Eve. He knew what to expect. Mother and I had talked of little else since Thanksgiving. He didn't object—how could he? One look at Barbara's dancing eyes and feet said it all.

Dad and Mother were in the kitchen, talking, catching up on the week. Barbara and I were under the tree, she on one side of the middle, me on the other. We were playing the game.

"Do you see the red ball?" I said. "Way, way up, near the top? Right next to the sleigh—there! See, the one with Santa Claus in it?" And I pointed.

"I see it, I see it!" Barbara said. "There it is, Joanie."

Dad had come into the room. He was standing quietly in the doorway. It crossed my mind that he had had a few too many bourbons without water. We had become very keen, Mother and I, on where Dad was in his drinking. It pretty much decided how we would spend our evening.

He saw my eyes watching him, and smiled, eyes first, then his mouth, and he took a step toward us, but then seemed to remember something that caused him to look away. He located his cigarettes and lighter on the end table, apparently what he came into the living room for. He picked them up and headed back toward the kitchen.

"That Daddy?"

"Never mind," I said. "It's Christmas."

And we looked back, deep into the tree.

I took her little hand in mine and everything shimmered and sparkled and shone.

PART TWO

Marvels

17

Ana

BARBA. BARBA," she said in a tiny flat voice as she walked through the kitchen to the deck door and out onto the deck.

I could hear her deep raspy breathing from the kitchen as I was cleaning up from snacktime. Ana was usually the last to finish whatever we were doing. She was calling Barbara, who was in the backyard with the other children, because she needed her overalls buttoned.

In between her calls I could hear her labored breathing. Because she had been very sick, she was quite young for her age. Her face and voice were without expression: her calling voice and her conversational were one and the same.

I was the only one who heard her. I said, "Ana, let me help you." She continued walking, calling in a monotone, "Barba. Barba," as if I wasn't there.

Ana hadn't spoken a word to me yet. When Barbara wasn't there, she patiently waited for her return. I, on the other hand, was becoming a bit impatient with her continued exclusion of me.

This is a funny little person, I thought to myself as I put the last dish in the drainer and wiped off the stove. She was $2\frac{1}{2}$ at the time. On the one hand, she was one of the most self-contained and self-controlled little girls I had ever had; on the other, as her pediatrician Dr. Samuels termed it, she was "socially inexperienced."

I was remembering her first interview with us. Since Timmy's time, we were diligent about interviewing parents and communicating with them at regular intervals. We talked at length about our approach to discipline, food, toilet training, and play. Barbara and I had become much clearer about what we actually do and skilled at articulating it to parents. This gave them something to respond to—to know if our approach is what they had in mind for their child.

I had also learned parents were our richest resource. They had the information, expertise, and insight about their child that we needed to do our job. So while I was telling them as much as I could about me, I was also learning as much as possible from them.

While the adults talked, Ana sat listlessly in a chair with tired eyes, a slack jaw, and her mouth open for breath. Clearly, she was not interested in anything in the playroom. Every once in a while she'd get up laboriously, come over to her father or mother, sit in one of their laps, lay her large head on their chests for a while, and then slowly crawl back down and over to her chair.

I didn't question the four days a week that her parents wanted with us. Frankly, I questioned taking her at all. She seemed slow to me, but perhaps, I thought, it was only because she was inexperienced. Born with an immune system that did not manufacture sufficient white blood cells, she had been in and out of hospitals, often with respiratory infections, and had come close to dying many times. At two, she had the developmental level in certain areas of a one-year-old. Her mother, Carrie, whom I greatly respected, had dedicated her life to this little girl. One of her pediatricians had wanted at birth to put her in a bubble to protect her. But Carrie believed that because Ana was a borderline case, perhaps if she were left out of a protective bubble she might at least have the opportunity to develop a stronger immune system. So she found a pediatrician who supported her journey to keep Ana, not only alive, but well.

During the interview, I felt her parents were so grateful she was alive—the slightest cold would often develop into pneumonia—that they were unaware of how lethargic and disinterested she was. At first, I thought she was just worn out, that was why she could barely keep her eyes open.

"Oh, no," Carrie said placidly. "This is how she always is."

Afterward, I was frankly surprised at how enthusiastic Barbara was about Ana coming.

"But are we capable of taking care of her? Here's a child, Barbara, who is going to need a *lot* from us." I expressed all my hesitancies. She had a lot of physical problems, she might be slow intellectually, she didn't know how to interact in a group. I ended with the fact that it didn't even seem as if she could breathe through her nose at all. "Did you hear her?" I asked. "I thought I was sitting by Darth Vader."

"Don't call her that," Barbara said as she stuck her chin up.

"But I'm afraid she doesn't have enough stamina to manage here. And if we have to give her a great deal of attention, won't we be taking from others?"

"Do we just take the strong?" she asked, standing up. Barbara is short with bright curly blond hair and very blue eyes. She was twenty-nine and had a kind of absolute faith in how destiny sometimes sends us a child. Her belief can be infuriating at times. "Is that it? Is that why we do all these screenings and interviews and phone calls? To ferret out only the perfect kid?"

"Of course not! But, Barbara, this little girl could get mortally sick and I'm worried about our other eleven. We might be taking from them." I still regretted how little time I was able to give to the other children when I had been working so exclusively with Timmy. And I felt that in the past I had bitten off more than I could chew. So why would I now choose that again?

"Then why do we have a place where we can give individual care and attention? What kind of care has she gotten so far? My God, Joan, this is her *fourth* daycare in six months!" She looked me straight in the eyes. *"I want to take her."*

"Okay," I said. "Okay." I trusted Barbara's intuition implicitly. "If you feel that strongly . . . Anyway, you've got a point, what *are* we about?"

The truth was that Barbara and I both knew that no other daycare would give her what we could here. She'd just be in four more daycares. "Okay," I said. "But this time, it's your turn."

18

Ana's First Day

ANA'S FIRST DAY WITH US, her mother brought her in carrying hiking boots, a down jacket, and a sweatshirt. Ana herself had on sweat pants, several layers of clothes, and tennis shoes. The day had been threatening rain and they wanted to be ready for any extremes of weather.

As I helped her mother find a place for all of Ana's things, I said, "We don't go outside in the rain, Carrie, so you won't have to bring all these clothes next time. And we'll be sure that she has on the right things."

"Oh," she said, dumbfoundedly. "At Ana's last daycare they were out in all kinds of weather. I found it difficult to anticipate just what that would mean so I got used to bringing everything!" And she laughed.

The first place Carrie had tried was Tinkerbelle's, a large "activity-based" nursery school with thirty-six children. That meant, every time a new activity was begun—such as finger

painting, dancing, reading, or crafts—every child participated. Ana was absolutely terrified there. All day long she sat
on a stool, fearful to get down on the floor. At night, she lay
in bed with her eyes open until sleep finally overcame her.
The three morning and three afternoon teachers thought she
was very strange.

Next Carrie put her in Rain Drops where the cribs were
stacked one upon the other and the children watched TV all
day. There Ana slept, but that's about all.

Finally, in desperation, Carrie tried the Drop Off Dump.
That name was really The Delightful Drop Off but the parents
nicknamed it Dump. It was a daycare cooperative, parent-
supported and -run. It turned out to be an Outward Bound
kind of program for two- to four-year-olds which depended
largely on field trips and a lot of volunteer parents to watch
over it. Daily, a group of twenty tots could be seen holding
onto a rope, being led down the streets of the city to visit
parks and museums and zoos. Ana was exhausted, over-
heated, cold, and wet after these journeys. And often the
day's busy schedule didn't allow for a nap.

For a little girl with health problems, this kind of daycare
sounds crazy. But her pediatrician, Dr. Samuels, felt that even
though Ana was very prone to infection, it was more important for her to spend time with children. And being cooped
up at home or at the hospital didn't help anyway: she was
still getting sick. So Carrie and Tom decided they were willing
to take the risk. Thankfully, by the third daycare, someone
told her about us, telling her that we were a gentle, protected
daycare without two sets of morning and afternoon teachers,
where the same people who said hello in the morning said
good-bye at night. And that above all, we supported children
to confidently manage their own lives.

Ana cried when her mother left that first day. But she
let me take her hand and we walked a few feet into the playroom. Several children were already there. Barbara was due
in about a half hour.

After a few more steps Ana stopped walking and dropped

my hand. She stood there until she was tired of standing and then she plopped down. She watched everything from this spot, breathing heavily from her mouth, never moving to get a toy or to explore and ignoring the toys I presented to her. She was right there in the doorway when Barbara came in.

She greeted Ana and the others and went into the kitchen to make breakfast. A short time later she called from the hall, "Breakfast is ready!" All the children hurried to the kitchen except Ana. She sat.

Well, an hour in one spot is enough, I thought.

I went to her, took her hand, and said, "Come with me, Ana. Barbara has made pancakes and eggs for us. Are you hungry?" She looked up at me and rose laboriously. Together we walked slowly into the kitchen.

The moment she realized what this was about—food— she dropped my hand, immediately got into the small vacant chair waiting for her, and grabbed her fork.

After each helping she would hold her plate up to Barbara for more food or her cup up for more juice. We ran out of scrambled eggs and Barbara finally stopped making more pancakes and refilling her cup after all the others had returned to their play.

I was relieved to find we offered something here that Ana wanted to do! I told Barbara later that Ana tolerated her more than me because she fed her first. But Barbara laughed and said, "No, it's because I'm more charming."

Ana stayed at the table while Barbara cleaned up. It was Barbara who led her back to the playroom. It began to rain, so I made a fire and asked the children to bring a book they wanted to hear. I began reading as Ana stood for a while where she was, letting go of Barbara's hand, and then finally sitting down, just outside our circle. A few children played with toys while most listened to the story. Barbara approached Ana several times in a friendly way, sometimes with a toy, sometimes with just a comforting word, but Ana remained where she was, watching.

It was Wednesday so Hildegard, our music teacher, came

with her accordion. The children sang songs and did some dancing. We scooted Ana over from the center of the room toward the fireplace. She sat there and watched until it was time for lunch. I made it and called the children.

Everyone came except Ana. "Ana, I made spaghetti and hot bread for lunch. Are you coming?" Nothing. I went to her and took her hand. She moved at my pace, breathing from her mouth, until the kitchen came into view. Then she let go of me and moved with a purpose to her chair, sat down, and looked toward Barbara. *I* serve lunch, however, and I served her first.

"Ana, what would you like on your plate?"

Silence.

"Spaghetti with sauce or plain, Ana?"

Silence.

I decided that if she spoke she would probably say "everything," so I served her spaghetti noodles with meat sauce and Parmesan cheese sprinkled on top and two pieces of hot French bread and butter. Barbara served her milk. She dug in.

I'm not sure how she managed, but Ana was the most efficient spaghetti eater I've ever seen. It all went into her mouth, not onto the table or the floor, in one steady, satisfying stream. She ate three plates' full with equal servings of French bread.

We washed up and had a story before naptime. Barbara called, "Naptime," and all but a few older children who didn't nap scurried about choosing what stuffed animal or book they would take to nap that day. Barbara took Ana's hand and led her to the playroom. She laid out mattresses and put down each child's blanket, bottle, if they took one, and particular sleep toy. She gently took off their shoes, covered them up, kissed them good night, and turned on a story record.

Ana was staring at her. Barbara smiled and looked at her in a comforting manner. She could have laid down beside her, stroked her hair or her back, but something said don't.

It was the same intuition that caused us both to take her by the hand all morning, rather than pick her up and hold her or carry her about. She went to sleep then, her face turned toward Barbara, her thumb in her mouth and the fingers of her other hand pulling and stroking the skin at her neck. She slept the whole naptime and when she woke, she allowed Barbara to put her shoes on and get her ready for snacktime.

All mealtimes were successes for Ana. She ate the cheese and fruit and crackers with gusto. Then we all settled in the playroom for the rainy afternoon. Her mother came and was pleased that we hadn't needed to call her. Ana had made it through her first day.

But afterward I looked at Barbara and shook my head. "This looks like a lot of work," I said, and then I laughed. "I hope you can handle it."

19

The Silent Treatment

SINCE THAT FIRST DAY, Ana still had not spoken a word to me. How much longer can she be content to always have to find Barbara or wait for her to be buttoned up or given something she can't reach? I mused as I swept the floor. At some point she will have to ask me.

I went outdoors. Ana was searching for something. I watched as she walked down the entire length of the yard and then across it. In the center we have a dome climber where several children were playing. As she continued to walk to and fro, I got closer. I could hear her. "Brambul. Brambul," she whispered. I could barely hear her call.

Bramble had become Ana's best friend. From the first she was very kind to her and later, when there was someone there inside Ana, she had a real friend.

That day, Bramble was one of the children climbing on the dome but I'm sure she didn't hear Ana's tiny whisper.

Ana must have passed her five times before Bramble happened to jump down in front of her and Ana saw her.

"Brambul," she said without expression. "I have found you." And her eyes sparkled with triumph as she threw her chubby arms out.

Even though Ana was two, she had the spatial gaps of a one-year-old: If she didn't see something it no longer existed. Also, her "window to the world" was barely open. When we say a child's window to the world is wide open we mean that he or she is alert and aware of all the stimuli coming in. In Ana's case, however, her window was open only to that which she could manage. It was hard for her to find people and things. She would trip over something she was looking for, get up, and keep on searching for it. If she didn't expect it to be there, she wouldn't see it.

As the days continued to go by, Ana's inability to do the simplest task for herself and her inability to find things continued to be difficult for her and for us. Early on we were certain that she would become motivated to reach out and ask for what she wanted. This didn't happen. I had the uneasy feeling that perhaps she couldn't. She seemed to be content to wander about until she bumped into something or someone that interested her. She cried when she hurt herself and laughed out loud at something funny. Otherwise, she was listless and lethargic most of the time, never frustrated or angry. She moved as she talked, at an even, purposeful rate. Her words lacked emotion. If her feelings were hurt she would try not to cry. Instead, she rubbed her eyes furiously and kept a stiff upper lip.

"Ana," I said. "What do you want?"

She had been having trouble fastening the strap of her overalls again when she finally bumped into me in the yard.

"Ana?" I said again. I wanted her to speak to me.

She just stuck her chest out.

"Oh," I said. "You want me to undo your strap? Okay, I will."

An hour later, I saw her in the yard. "Hi," I said and she ignored me.

"Oh, that's not going to work," I said, smiling. "When I say hi to you, I want you to say hi to me. I don't want you to turn away." She looked at me with no expression whatsoever and walked away.

20

I Find Out

EANWHILE, JEFFIE'S WITHDRAWAL CONTINUED and I didn't know what to do. I felt in a real quandary because on the one hand, Rolph was telling me his withdrawing from us was serious and I needed to bring him back by play. On the other hand, Jeffie had made it very clear that he didn't want me to.

At this time, my deepest intuition began to tell me that there was a way of being with him which didn't mean playing on his level, but was a way of melding with or of supporting him on perhaps even a more profound level. It had happened to me a few times before with a child. It was a kind of being in tune, however briefly, that would leave each of us with a feeling of comfort and of trust.

One of those times it happened to me was with Bramble. When she first came she was always just so. She was a prim little girl who wore neat braids and matching outfits and she began most sentences with, "In the Stringer household, we don't—"

From the moment she arrived, she didn't want to be here. She would say to her mother, "I don't want to stay; it smells."

Her mother would say comforting things and leave. Bramble wouldn't cry; rather, she remained aloof, detached really, and totally unaccepting of me and everyone else.

She called me teacher. She was $2\frac{1}{2}$, very bright, and too skilled in putting everything down.

"In the Stringer household," Bramble sniffed one day, looking at Sandy, "we don't have dirty dogs." One day Barbara made a favorite pancake recipe. "In the Stringer household, we eat only waffles."

Yet each morning, I'd greet her at the door with, "Bramble, I am happy to see you. Come, let's find something to do!"

"Teacher," she'd pout, "your blouse is messy."

Then one day, at about eleven o'clock in the morning she started screaming at the top of her lungs. She had a terrible earache. Earaches often come on like that in a little child. I called her mother at work. She said, "I'll come as soon as possible." She told me to give her some baby aspirin. She was going to come and take her immediately to the doctor.

Bramble was in terrible pain as she took the baby aspirin I gave her. I told her her mother was coming so she had some relief. I was holding her in my arms and walking around with her but she struggled to get out. Once on the floor she was unhappy too. So I picked her up and said, "Let's go out on the front deck and wait for them." I took the rocker and I pulled it onto the deck and shut the front door. She and I sat on the deck as near as we could to the street so that she could watch for her mother. And I rocked and rocked her and in that rocking something happened. She engaged with me from that time on.

One day not long afterward, while I was at the stove, I

spilled a ladle of spaghetti sauce on myself. "Oops," I exclaimed. "That certainly wouldn't have happened in the Stringer household, would it, Bramble?" I turned around and smiled.

She was sitting at the little table behind me. "Oh, Joanie," she said laughing. "This is the Stringer household now sort of, isn't it?"

One day, I was out in the yard and I noticed that Jeffie had broken a toy that he loved. It was a little blower, like a party favor, not made to last, but he loved this thing. It had a feather on its end and it came back when you blew it. Well, it had lost its feather in a fight with Timmy D. long ago. He didn't like that much, but he had accepted that fact. And now he was alone in his corner trying to blow it. And it wouldn't blow anymore.

Ordinarily I wouldn't repair it. I would tell a child, "Look, this is the way these things are." But I needed some contact with this little boy.

I went over to him and I said, "Well, let's see, maybe if I put some tape on it, maybe it will work." And I spent what he realized was a lot of time trying to fix this simple thing. And I fixed it. I asked him to blow it and it worked.

I took it back, looked it over, and said, "It isn't going to last very long but we fixed it for the moment."

Jeffie looked at me with those sparkling eyes of his, lifted his thick eyebrows, and said, "When Greeney fixes things for me, they never break!"

"Greeney?" I asked. "Who's Greeney?"

"Greeney's my shark!" he said, taking his blower from my hands. "And he's going to *get* you!" And he blew it in my face and ran off.

21

Ana Dancing

THEN ONE MORNING, Carrie brought Ana as usual. She stood still, looking out toward the play yard while her mother took off her coat. As soon as she was free, she lumbered outside. Carrie turned to me excitedly and said, "Ana must be really doing things here. You're having dancing?"

"Dancing?" To my knowledge Ana hadn't participated in any musical activities at our house since she had come. As usual, she would plop down on the floor and watch all the children.

"Ana is *dancing* at home!"

I was stunned. Carrie went on to tell me that each day when Ana came home from nursery school, she made her mother, father, and their friends sit down while she sang and danced for them.

Are we talking about the same child? I wondered, looking over at Ana, slack-jawed, sitting on the edge of the bark box.

"In fact," she went on, "I've just come from Dr. Samuels's office where Ana did a dance for him." She smiled delightedly. "Two months ago, Joan, she used to see him and scream! You are working marvels with this girl!"

Marvels?

Then she went on to tell me something even more extraordinary. Ana had told Dr. Samuels that she didn't want to be sick anymore.

"I want to go to Joanie and Barbara's," she said.

"You do?" he asked. And with tears in his eyes he told Carrie that this was the most wonderful thing he could ever have wished for for Ana.

"Marvels!" her mother said as she walked out. "You and Barbara are working marvels."

I watched her go. Marvels, I thought. Carrie had just given me vital information about Ana. Clearly, talking with parents worked both ways.

Meanwhile, Ana still had not spoken a word to me.

The next day, once again, Ana needed her overall straps buckled. I was alone with her in the kitchen, cleaning up. She looked toward the outside where Barbara was and then at me. I understood her dilemma. If she asked me to help she wouldn't have to shuffle all the way through the kitchen, outside across the deck, down the deck stairs, across the play yard to Barbara standing by the sandbox. While she knew enough to hold the straps in her hand, she hadn't yet learned to pull the overalls up to her waist and hold them there. They were still around her ankles. But if she asked me, she would have to speak to me.

I thought, "Okay, Ana, be very careful what you choose, because this is a deciding factor in our relationship. If you ask me for help, I *won't* let you *not* respond to me again."

She looked at me, deciding.

I looked at her challengingly.

She shuffled toward me, stood still, held out her strap, and said, "Do this."

"I will be happy to do this for you, Ana," I said. "And from now on we are going to talk to each other."

I buckled her up and demanded, "Now say thank you." She did and went out of doors. I usually don't demand please, thank you, and you're welcome in this parroting manner with children at all. But I wanted Ana to say something else to me and it was the only thing I could think of at the time.

"Marvels," I thought to myself, laughing. "If her mother only knew . . ." Then I thought again, "Marvels."

22

Orangey

HAD TO LAUGH, ROLPH, when she thought Barbara and I were
some sort of miracle workers!" I was back in Rolph's too-
small office. Too neat. Too . . . "I can't do it," I said,
interrupting myself. "I know you think it is right, but I
can't engage with Jeffie on that level."

"But why not? You've tried everything else and now
you have the beginning of some rapport with him again—"

"Very, very fragile rapport."

"But an opening nonetheless." He wiped his nose with
a monogrammed handkerchief. "I think you should take it."

"Take what?"

"Take the opening and create some sort of imaginary
playmate—something—he has a green shark, you can have a
. . . an orange one!"

"I don't know."

But the truth was, my way wasn't working. I could be
with that child all day long and unless he wanted to share

with me, there was nothing I could do. I had met Greeney only one other time. When I was crossing the play yard one day, Jeffie came careening down the walk on his trike saying, "Watch out! Greeney will get you!" I jumped back out of his way and he laughed.

"Nancy," I said, catching her as she was going out the door. "Do you know much about this playmate of Jeffie's? This Greeney? His shark?"

"Oh, yes, he always has Greeney with him. Before that was Truckie."

"Truckie?"

She leaned against the doorjamb with her purse tucked under her arm. "Remember when I was doing volunteer work at that battered women's center?"

"Yes?"

"Well, I used to take Jeffie with me every night and we'd be in a hurry and going through traffic and he created Truckie to knock the cars out of my way. When someone impolitely got in front of me in my lane, he used Truckie to get him out!"

"Oh," I said. "Well, I've been noticing that he has gotten much quieter lately, even withdrawn."

"Really? I know he's certainly easier to be with." She smiled.

"I've been thinking that might be where he has gone—that he's Greeney."

"I don't know. I know Truckie was certainly useful; but listen, I have to rush—I trust you know what you're doing. He's a changed boy since he's been here."

"Yeh," I said, thinking that he had changed perhaps not for the better, so different from Ana who was progressing on a road I could clearly see and understand. I didn't feel that what Jeffie was going through was progress. It seemed odd to me and out of character.

"Just think, Joan, only one pluggie to bother with now!"

she said as she left. "He used to be hysterical if he misplaced one! And no more gigantic green airplane to carry around everywhere he went besides that dirty blanket of his."

"Ah ha," I said. "He's certainly traveling lighter."

I got the feeling that Nancy didn't want to hear any troubling news about her son. This made sense to me. She had just gone through such trauma with her divorce and done so much soul-searching about Jeffie already. Barbara and I had met with Nancy and her ex-husband and their new partners and talked extensively about what was best for Jeff. She was happy to do everything we suggested and had developed great trust in me.

I just wish I felt the same trust in myself, I thought, as I watched her go.

One day, I went over to Jeffie as he played as usual alone in the play yard and I said, "Orangey wants to play."

His back was to me and he turned around abruptly. His hair was shorter now but he still had his Groucho eyebrows. They shot up in delight. "Orangey?" he said smiling. "Greeney wants to play." He walked toward me.

"Are you Orangey?"

"Yes," I nodded.

"You want to play, Orangey?"

"Yes," I said.

"Really?" he said, his face delighted. I tried to smile. Then he hunkered down on his knees and he pulled me down with him. "Now Jeffie," I said. "Anything that happens here is okay. Nobody's bad, nobody's to blame, afterward you and I are the same, okay?" He looked at me. "Don't be afraid, Joanie."

I swallowed. "Okay."

"Come on," he said. "We're swimming in a dark blue sea and you're Orangey and I'm after you and you're running away and I'm going to bite you in half with my teeth and both parts of you are going to swim away and I'll be mixed up which one to catch but because I'm very powerful and very fast and have a very big and dangerous mouth—" His eyes were huge and his eyebrows almost up into his hair. "— And a very big tail. I'll get both halves of you, so watch out! Here I come."

And so we began to play. Once Jeffie began to share Greeney with me around Orangey, he was very open about him. I learned all the details. He was all-powerful and particularly liked to cut people in half and save women and children from bad men. This is where he had been the last few months. It fit perfectly with what his mother had to tell me about visiting the battered women's shelter. He knew that some men were very bad and Greeney could help women and give them IVs and cut the bad men into little bitty pieces.

After that he began to run around the yard saying to other kids, "You want some help? Greeney'll get them for you!"

Every time he and I played Orangey and Greeney, he would always say something like, "Okay, I'm going to play with Greeney and you're going to play with Orangey." And I would say, "And when we're through playing, it won't matter what we did, because it's all pretend, right, Jeffie?"

"Right."

"I'm going to be Joanie playing with Greeney and you're Jeffie playing with Orangey, okay?"

"Okay."

And then we would begin. We would always be swimming in a dark blue sea and he would be after me and he would be saying things like, "I'll put out your eyes, cut off your ears, and stuff them in your mouth! I'll pull out every bit of your hair and take your legs and twist them off and bang them against a tree!"

There was so much volatile and violent energy for Jeffie in this play that sometimes it made me uneasy. It didn't scare the other children, though. They watched but got bored. You see, for them cut-up people can be put back together. It's no big deal.

But for me, it was a big deal. Greeney was so real for Jeffie. He did whatever Jeffie needed him to do. He was invincible. He could knock cars off the freeway for Nancy, he could save women and children from bad men who hit them; he was a definite power.

One day as we started to play, I listened carefully to his exact words, "We're going into the water now. And I'm going to play with Greeney and you're going to play with Orangey and when we're through you'll be Joan playing with Orangey."

I said, "Why can't I *be* Orangey if you get to be Greeney?" For I realized that what he was saying was that I couldn't be Orangey, that I was only manipulating him.

Jeffie looked at me absolutely stunned. "I'm not Greeney," he said.

"Why not?" I asked.

"I'm not Greeney," he said and walked quickly away.

23

Getting Greeney

H E'S NOT REALLY GREENEY," I said to Rolph from the phone in my bedroom.

"What?" Rolph said.

"He manipulates Greeney, but Greeney's separate from him."

"Joan," he said. "This doesn't sound good."

"Why?" I asked. "Isn't it a good thing—I mean, then he's just an imaginary playmate like many children have all the time."

"Because I don't think that this is such a healthy place for Jeff to be. Greeney, for him, is all the emotions and all the violence and he takes all the responsibility. Not Jeffie. But there's a catch here . . ."

"What?" I held the phone tightly in my hand.

"From what you've told me, Jeffie is aware of the fact that he is the one who controls Greeney. That's why it's not going to work. Jeffie has to own his own feelings, Joan. Greeney the shark is the subtotal of Jeffie's emotions right this moment. Now he'll tell you anything about Greeney you want to know; the only trouble you're going to have is getting him to *be* Greeney."

"I can't do that," I said emphatically. "I've told you before, I'm not comfortable manipulating his play like that."

"Once he's Greeney you accept him," Rolph went right on, "which you're going to do because you already know he's Greeney and you accept him. You see, he's the one who's got to find this out."

"I don't want to directly intervene in his fantasy," I said.

"Joan, why don't you come in the office and we'll discuss this?"

"I can't. I don't have a second this week, Laura has an art show and Karen is—"

"All right, we'll do it here on the phone right now." He was silent for a moment. I could hear the children playing outside. Thank God Barbara was there to relieve me. I had to make this phone call. "What is standing in your way of really helping this boy?"

"Are you certain that he can manage all of these feelings if we force him to own them?" I asked. "Because that's what we're down to. I know how volatile his fantasies with Greeney are. This kid is a volcano of anger—he wants to cut up everyone who he considers mean and nasty, from Timmy D. to all the bad men who batter women to the cars on the freeway that cut in front of his mother. I'm just worried about him becoming Greeney and being one with all this violence."

"Jeffie created Greeney, Joan," Rolph said slowly as if he were speaking to someone very dense. "Greeney is the repository of all his feelings and all his fantasies. Greeney's the one who's done the dismembering, Greeney's the one who protects people. Didn't you tell me that he protects some people?"

"Yes."

"Jeffie needs to step inside and *be* Greeney and then he can be Jeffie again. Greeney is how Jeffie has worked out all his problems. The minute Jeffie becomes Greeney he is going to *know* that he is actually the one who acted on everything and all these problems with Jeffie that you're discussing are going to be solved."

"Really?" I said, quite amazed. "Do you really think this is so? What I fear is that I'll deny him the comfortable situation he is in. You know yesterday he stopped me on the deck. I was hurrying around trying to get a birthday party together and he said, 'Don't worry, Joanie. The waters ahead are safe. Greeney's here.' And then he helped set out the plates. Extraordinary things have happened with this boy since Greeney."

"You're wrong," he said. "This boy isn't comfortable, he's very uncomfortable."

"How do you know this?" I said, annoyed and suddenly diffident.

"I know he's not comfortable with these feelings because he has had to manufacture a fantasy character to contain them."

"But perhaps he really needs this comfort for a while. This fantasy comes from inside him." I was frowning. "Anyway, how is Greeney different from Jennifer's fantasy about her doll living here? Or Timmy playing baby? He believed he was a baby when he was in that cradle."

"Neither of them totally lived in their fantasy for months nor were they so dissociated from them nor were they so violent. It is dangerous. He told you that. He is too detached. You know that, that's what you first said to me. His play is far away. So detached. Anytime there is a big change in a child, like with Jeffie, when he has lots of problems, and suddenly, all by himself, he becomes content, you need to worry."

"Why? Maybe he's found religion."

"Joan," Rolph said patiently. "This isn't funny. What you need to be aware of, when you're out there negotiating around in the waters, being Orangey and Greeney, is any furtive looks around—watch for them and support him at these times—say to him nothing's changed, everything's okay."

Nancy knew a lot about Orangey and Greeney because they were everywhere now in Jeffie's life. He talked about what Greeney did all the time. "You know that Timmy, Mom? If that Timmy were here Greeney'll sure get him—Greeney'll beat him to a pulp and then eat him for breakfast!" "Don't worry, Mom, Greeney will take care of it—Greeney can do anything!" "Mom, Mom! Greeney flew today! Isn't that great? He doesn't need water to be strong, no sir!" And on and on.

He felt so confident about Greeney. He wanted everybody to know about him. Greeney was his friend. He was an invincible shark and Jeffie was quite content with that.

Nancy and I worked out a rather clear picture of Greeney. He was bigger than anyone else and he didn't really need water to swim in. Sometimes he could fly. Sometimes Jeffie could see him, sometimes not. It didn't matter to him at all whether we could see him or not. Greeney was always there and that's what mattered. And Jeffie could do anything because of Greeney. The waters ahead were safe because of him.

Nancy was no more concerned about Greeney than she had been about Truckie, the white truck. And since I was so mixed up about my concerns and unclear about Rolph's fears, I didn't have a coherent statement to make to Nancy about Greeney.

"Joan," Nancy said. "You do what you need to do. I trust you totally. Everything you have told me to do with Jeffie has worked. I know you'll do the best for him."

"All my instincts tell me not to do this with Jeffie, Carol." We were up in my room sipping wine. Laura and Karen had taken charge of Carol's daughter Tina for the evening.

She knew what I was talking about. We had talked of nothing else for days.

"But then I ask myself, why am I in supervision if it's not to get some guidance on what to do?"

"Right. *And* Rolph did help you with Timmy."

"That he did. And the extreme change in Jeffie has bothered me."

"That's why you went to an expert."

"Is he?"

"Joan. At some point you have to trust someone."

I sighed and stared into my wineglass. I sloshed its contents around. I felt so unprofessional whenever I talked to Rolph. He always had to analyze my feelings and then Timmy D.'s and Jeffie's behavior. It felt too much like therapy to me. And I wanted supervision, not therapy. I thought about it for a moment. I realized the person I had to learn to trust was myself.

"And besides," Carol said. "What I've always thought is that intervention can only bring about positive results unless it is not right for the child."

"That's true. And I don't think Jeffie will let me do it unless it is right for him."

24

The Yellow Chair

WELL, WHAT DOES ANA REALLY LOVE TO DO?'' We were trying to figure out some easy starter task that Ana could master.

"Why not putting her coat on?"

Barbara shook her head. "Too difficult."

Recently her parents told us that Ana cried on Saturdays and Sundays because she couldn't come to our place. That, coupled with the fact that she was finally talking to me, made Barbara and me feel that we were on firmer ground with her. She was ready to take on new challenges and learn how to take matters into her own hands.

Barbara and I were eating a barbecued chicken after work from Ranzanto's down the street. "I know," I said. "She loves food and meals—"

"Right," Barbara said. "We can find something for her to do around food."

"What if we had her find her own chair every time she ate?"

Barbara nodded. "That just might work."

The next day, Barbara called, "Breakfast," and the children scurried into the kitchen. Ana continued to fold a blanket over her dolly. She liked to finish things. She never scurried but walked with enthusiasm into the kitchen. Everyone was seated and Ana had a place but no chair.

"Barbara," she said, looking up. "Chair."

"Ana," Barbara said. "Go get one from the other room."

Ana didn't argue. She walked into the playroom and as I watched, she circled it, looking for the chair.

As she continued to circle and circle the playroom, I asked, "What are you doing?"

She said, "Chair."

The little lightweight chair was bright yellow. She had passed within an inch of it several times. Then she saw it. She was thrilled.

"I found it," she said in her monotone.

"That you did," I said.

Then she looked at it. Tried to pick it up, but couldn't. She looked at it again and then over at me.

"Drag it from the back," I said.

She looked at it.

"I'll show you," I said.

Though she had done this for short distances in the past, for the children were always dragging these chairs from room to room depending on what game they were playing, I wasn't surprised that she hadn't thought of it now. It seemed different to transport the chair all the way to the kitchen than just to move it a few feet.

I tilted it back so she could place her hand on it, and then she started walking backward. It took a very long time to do it this way, pulling the chair, but I left further instructions unsaid. I decided to appreciate her way.

She finally arrived in the kitchen huffing, puffing, happy to have done what Barbara and I asked.

*   *   *

There is always a strong temptation to do things for children when you work with a large group day in, day out. It's so much easier, and even sometimes better for the group, if the grown-ups help children put their shoes and coats on. It seems to take forever when we let them do it themselves. Yet, for us to button, zip, buckle, and tie for every child instead of giving them enough time to do it for themselves robs children of myriad valuable experiences.

It means, though, that we are always having to concentrate on their pace and the importance of letting each child achieve whatever he or she can. Barbara and I knew that in order for Ana to mature we had to be particularly conscious of this with her. She needed so much help that it was a real temptation to do it for her, rather than support her efforts to do it for herself.

Yet, to be honest, my instinct was to say, "Look—this is how you do it," but I knew that was not what we could do here. We had to stand back and support her in her own efforts.

I would have to wait at least twenty minutes while Ana figured out her right and left shoes. She did this entirely by feel. She almost always chose the wrong shoe and so put both shoes on wrong. She'd stand up—I'd think to myself, thank God—start walking, stop and say, "No."

Sitting back down, she'd start all over again. Sometimes she'd laboriously take both shoes off, put them on again, and still have them on the wrong feet! But oh her joy, and *mine,* when she got them right!

Allowing Ana her very slow pace was difficult but we got so much from her when she succeeded. Ana's joy at being able to do it for herself was an unexpected reward. She had so much energy for living. She made it worth it for us in a way that no other child has done.

The littlest thing could just delight her. And you wanted to be with her because you wanted some of it to rub off on you—the perfect day, how rain felt on her face, seeing some wonderful thing—a tightly curled leaf, a new pair of shoes. When Ana got new shoes, and after she finally got them on the right feet, she would just sit there and rock back and forth and look at her new shoes and just be amazed.

25

The Bark Box

ONE AFTERNOON, energized by Ana's success with the yellow chair, I said to her, as she fell over the border of the bark box—a container full of redwood chips—for the eightieth time, "Ana, someday you'll walk right across the yard into the bark box and out without even falling."

"Really," she said happily. "Will you show me how?"

"Of course."

The next day was glorious, sunny without a cloud in sight. Usually we get more fog, which I like because I get to make a summer fire. We had our breakfast juice and toast out on the deck. Ana came over to me. "Let's do the bark box."

"Okay, hold my hand."

On and off all morning, we practiced getting into and out of the bark box. However, whenever we weren't practicing I noticed that every time Ana would get in or out of the bark box, she'd trip.

Throughout that week, we continued. I became increasingly discouraged and frustrated. Into, out of, lift your feet, that's it, into, out of, out of, into, good, Ana! Then five minutes later, on her own, she'd trip as she ran to get into it. I found myself thinking mean thoughts: Pick up your feet! Or, don't use the bark box, then, go around it! No one is *this* clumsy, you're doing it on purpose! Or maybe, I thought, if she really hurt herself, she'd learn! But I never said a word aloud. If she was able to try again and again so was I. Only occasionally, I'd say to her when she came up, ever cheerful and smiling, wanting to practice again for the twelfth time that day, "No—not now!"

It was her innocence that made me fall in love with her. How hard it was for her to do the littlest thing and how willing she was to try. That's the thing about Ana.

And then, one day, she did it! On her own, she stepped over the border of the bark box without tripping. And she was *thrilled!*

And so was I!

26

The Confrontation
with Greeney

KEPT SAYING TO MYSELF, as I walked toward him across the
yard, "This is what he really wants to do. Rolph's right.
This is what he really wants to do. He's uncomfortable.
He's—"

"Hi, Joanie!" he said and he just beamed. He was
growing so tall now, he looked like Ichabod Crane at four.
His eyebrows shot up. "Gee, you know where Greeney took
me last night? He took me to the most wonderful cave, it was
filled with little tiny—"

"Let's play Orangey and Greeney."

"Wow! Sure!" Jeffie was always up for Orangey and
Greeney. He jumped out of his car and followed me to the
"way back," the second area of our play yard, in back, away
from everyone else.

I structured the play as usual. "Okay," I said. "You're
going to play with Greeney, and I'm going to play with Orangey, and when we're through, it doesn't matter what we

did, because it was all pretend. I'm going to be Joan and not her playing with Orangey, and you're going to be Jeffie and not be playing with Greeney."

"Right," he said, beaming, wiping his nose, and nodding his shiny dark hair.

I got down near him and I whispered, "I want to do something different today."

"Okay!" he said, still smiling. "Orangey wants to be in the sky?" he whispered.

"Not this time," I said quietly. "Today I want to *be* Orangey, right here."

"NO," he said. And he stepped back.

"Yes," I said, louder. "Today I want to be Orangey. It's my game too. And I want you to *be* Greeney."

"I don't want to." He looked scared and started to back away again.

"I do," I said.

He stopped moving and considered. "Joanie?" he said. "This isn't a good idea. You know Greeney can get Orangey."

"I'm not worried about that. You know I can take care of myself."

"But I *don't* want to do it that way."

"I *do*. This is the way I want to do it." I stared at him. Either yes or no.

He had stopped backing away and he no longer looked scared. He was just standing there, holding his own, arguing with me. At that moment, I suddenly *knew* it was all right. I knew he wanted to do this and that it was up to me. If he didn't, you see, he would have already been gone.

"We're going to do it today," I said with more confidence, standing up. "We're going to start now. Come on. We're in the water. I'm Orangey and you're Greeney and I can take care of myself, Jeffie."

"I don't want to go in the water."

"Come on!" I said. "We're in the water, and you're going to be Greeney and I'm going to be Orangey and when this is over with, you're going to be Jeffie and I'm going to be Joanie and we're going to be here in the yard and we won't play anymore."

He moved toward me. "When it's over with—?" he said, interested. "I'm going to be Jeffie and you're going to be Joanie?"

"Yes," I said. "That's how it's going to be. But right now, I really want you to be Greeney."

And he stood in the middle of that dirt yard and I could see the concentration on his face. He was on the verge. A bluejay flew by.

He wanted to be Greeney but he was frightened.

"I'm Greeney," he said, his voice full of awe.

"Good!" I said quickly. "And I'm Orangey and we're going along, swimming along. Come on, start swimming with me." We started swimming together. "And you're much stronger than I am, you're Greeney and more powerful—"

Jeffie bared his teeth. "I'm bigger than you! I've got sharp teeth and a long tail and I can do whatever I want to do! I'm the fastest, the biggest, the most powerful shark around!"

And so we swam together once around that dirt yard. And then Jeffie stopped. He did not attack me at all. He walked away.

I watched him go back into the other yard. He had become Greeney and that was the end of it forever.

A few days later, Barbara asked him playfully, "Where's Greeney?"

"Greeney's dead," he said.

27

The Sand Castle

ONE DAY ANA was in the sandbox with three of her friends—Bramble, Mary, and Sally. The sand was damp enough toward the bottom of the box from the rain the night before. She had spent hours with us learning all about how to deal with wet sand. She was the master here, the knowledgeable one. She was delighted by the wet sand and determined to teach her friends all that she knew.

"Now, this dry sand," Ana said, pushing it away. "Here wet sand." She looked at them. "You don't know how to do this." With her hand on her chest, she said, "I do." Her friends were interested. "Watch."

Ana got a small plastic container and a large plastic bucket. She filled the larger container with a shovel. The others searched around for shovels and pails.

Ana said, "You're not watching. Watch!"

"We want to do it too," Bramble said.

"You can't. I show you how," Ana said determinedly. Her voice had become a little louder but still didn't express much emotion.

Ana's pace was very methodical. Her breathing had become much quieter by now but she was still slow. I could tell by the way her eyes darted here and there that she was hurrying. But since only her eyes were hurrying, she was quickly losing her students. Bramble and Mary were talking about swinging. Sally was leaning toward them. Ana, by this time, hadn't even begun to fill up the larger container.

I knew exactly what she was going to do. First fill the large container, tap it out to keep it firm, and then do the same with the smaller one on top. Then the fun begins. Is it a two-tiered cake? Decorate it. Is it a two-story building? Make windows and doors. Is it a castle? Use little square forms to make turrets. But Bramble, Mary, and Sally had already left for the swing.

I went over to the sandbox. Ana's eyes filled with tears. I said, "Finish it, Ana, it takes time to do these things. You can show them when you're finished."

She thought about it, threw the container, and said, "They don't want to play."

"Yes, they do want to play," I said. "They don't want to just watch. Next time let them handle the sand."

"They don't know how."

"They will learn by watching you and playing with the sand at the same time."

"Oh." She had thrown the container so she didn't have to cry. Ana had learned something.

28

Rolph Comes to Visit

I T WAS SATURDAY AGAIN. All the floors were vacuumed and clean, the toys washed and neatly put back in their place. I had just arranged a bouquet of wild roses and Canterbury bells in the dining room. Barbara and I had transformed the smaller playroom into a dining room by unfolding my teak desk into a table and by setting it for six, candles and all. I was having a dinner party that night, but this morning Rolph was coming to see our place and have lunch.

I was excited about having him here. All these months and he had never really seen our place. Everything he knew about it was from me. I knew when he got a feel of it he would see how really competent in my work I was. I always felt like such an idiot in his office.

He looked enormous standing in the doorway wearing a cardigan sweater and tie, his hand brushing his beard as always. He wanted to see the place before we ate.

As he walked around the playroom he said, "Don't you have any guns or swords?"

"Guns?" I said. "Swords?"

"Yes—children, boys and girls—need *aggressive* toys." His thick hands fingered this, picked up that, and put it down. He smiled. "I think if you had had more aggressive toys for Tim, he would have calmed down quicker."

"Timmy?" I said as I followed him around. Although Rolph was being gentle, I didn't like how he was picking up each toy and commenting on it. "Aggression," he said. "You need to help them get it out with less childish toys."

"Oh," I said.

Then we ate. I had invited Barbara to come but she was busy. It was a delicious lunch—good handmade pasta from down the street, a wonderful crisp Caesar salad, and a good wine.

We talked about Barbara and my work with Ana and I shared with him how we work with a child who's sick. "Essentially it's no different from that of working with an adult—that one needs to feel responsible for one's own illness," I said. "This is your body, your medicine, your health, or your ill health. This same attitude can be used with a very young child also. Before Ana came we had a little two-year-old boy who had diabetes and was medicated for it here. Whenever the medicine wore off, he became very thirsty. This was the signal he used to ask us for more medicine. We treated him as a normal child. It became no big deal for him. He took responsibility for these differences in himself." I got up and poured some more wine. "So too with Ana. I asked her mother if there was anything we needed to do in the way of physical care for her and she said, 'Nothing. She gets vitamins at home. She loves food. I know you serve natural foods here. She'll have a nap—treat her like you would any kid.' And so we have. Even though she has spatial gaps and breathing problems, we expect her to do what everybody does; it just takes longer."

Then he asked about Jeffie, as he wiped his mouth and

beard, and I found myself crying. "I'm sorry, Rolph," I said. "I certainly don't want this to turn into a session."

"What's up?" he said gently.

"I don't know," I shook my head. "He's certainly himself again—small and vulnerable and needy. Last week, he said he didn't like to play anymore because no one would do it his way."

"Well," he said, "he's right where he's supposed to be now, isn't he?"

"Yes," I said, blowing my nose. "Angry, getting his feelings hurt, jumping up and trying again, playing with a lot of kids now. A typical four-year-old, soon to be graduating from daycare into kindergarten."

"Then why are you crying?"

"Because I took away his Greeney." I wiped my eyes. "I know that sounds silly but I can't help remember how content and powerful he felt when he had his shark. 'The waters ahead are safe now,' he said. 'Greeney's here.' And I took that from him. It makes me feel sad."

"He wouldn't have grown out of Greeney, Joan."

"Yes," I nodded, and even though I didn't agree, going along with Rolph once again.

"You know we made the right decision because he so effortlessly let you in, right? No furtive looks, no struggle, nothing. He became Greeney and it all went away."

I started clearing away the dishes. "That's true." I sat down again, pulled out a Kleenex, and wiped my eyes. "I feel sad when I see this vulnerable little boy crying with his friends. Isn't that silly?"

When he left, I went back into the playroom to carefully put away all the toys Rolph had looked at. I love these toys, I thought, almost as much as I love this house. Barbara and I carefully choose each one. We replace them when they're damaged and we buy two or three of many of the favorites. These are the objects we live with twenty-four hours a day.

"Guns," I said aloud. I don't want to be surrounded with guns and aggressive toys. And I thought of Bozo and that hitting bag that I got Timmy D. How successful *that* was! It was the gift of language that calmed him down, I thought, and play. Gentle play. Timmy D. didn't choose war.

And suddenly I understood what I was feeling. As Rolph was walking around my place telling me about this toy and that, I felt like Ana in the sandbox. I wanted to stop him and say, "You don't know how to do this." And tap my chest. "I do. Watch me."

I laughed to myself. What a fool. It was clear that Rolph didn't know much about daycare. He may have a Ph.D., he may know something about kids, he may even have helped me and been insightful, but he didn't know a thing about what *I* did.

And I was content never to call him again.

29

Ana Crying

SALLY, MARY—WE'LL PLAY DOLLS NOW," Ana called very authoritatively to two of her friends.

They wanted to play. They had their dolls. Ana's plan was to lay them out on blankets that she chose. But Mary and Sally were already in the blanket basket choosing their own.

"No, no!" Ana cried out strictly. "I'll do that!"

"But we're already doing it, Ana," Mary said.

"Yeah, we're getting ours," Sally smiled. "Ana—here's one for you."

Tears quickly came into Ana's eyes and just as quickly up came two little hands to rub them away. She clamped her mouth shut but still trembled with hurt and disappointment. She had had a plan to organize the play. When she went forth to do it her friends wouldn't follow suit. She was stunned. It hurt her feelings. She always played their way, why wouldn't they play hers?

"Ana," I said, going to her. She let me hold her now.
"Ana, you're upset."

More tears, more rubbing of two little eyes, more muffled sobs.

"Don't cry, Ana."

Ana crying, as Barbara took her from me, holding her in
her arms and walking about, cooing, "Ana, Ana, Ana."

Finally, she sucked her thumb, pulled her neck, and qui-
eted down. She didn't express anger yet, or retaliation. But
she was finished playing dolls with Mary and Sally for the
time being.

By this time Ana had been with us for six months. She
was becoming part of a group of five $2\frac{1}{2}$-year-old girls who
would have a real impact on our daycare. During this time,
Ana had the beginnings of a cold several times. Dr. Samuels
would prescribe an antibiotic and decongestant. Ana, according to her mother, would stamp her foot and say, "I am not
sick! I want to go to Joanie and Barbara's!" Prior to being
with us, a runny nose or temperature had been a signal of
illness that always led to respiratory infection and a stay in
the hospital.

Carrie's almost freight train determination about Ana and
her accepting quality helped account for Ana's patient drive
about making it in the present.

For me, this transformation caused wonder. While before her entire face was expressionless, now her smile was
electrifying. We began to see the innocent, benign, cooperative, ever good side of Ana.

Flying high on her newfound knowledge after she
learned about the chair and the bark box, she went ahead
and made us teach her to pump on the swing, climb the dome
climber, butter her own bread, cut her own sandwich, dress
the dolls, use the toilet, brush her hair, make sand houses,
and everything else. We became aware of the shift in who

was the initiator of tasks and liked it. And with her peers, she began to initiate for the first time her ideas for play.

This is why it was quite a setback for Ana when her friends didn't follow her plan. It took her three days before she tried again. This time she had the same straightforward and purposeful voice but it was a bit softer. At our daycare, Ana was learning she needed others for the first time.

30

Ana Running

WHEN OTHER CHILDREN RAN, they always left Ana behind. She didn't seem to mind much, only wanting to catch up. The limits of the yard insured that she would. She walked, hopped a little, walked, hopped a little, but she never attempted running. We surmised that the abundance of scar tissue in her lungs from all her respiratory infections kept her from running like the others.

I was sitting on a lawn chair with a full view of the length of the sidewalk. It is almost as long as the backyard, which is about 100 feet. Out of the corner of my eyes, I noticed Ana. And what I noticed, riveted me to her.

There she came, long blond hair flying around her shoulders and streaming out behind. Arms straight out, not in front, but to each side, as if she were playing airplane, one foot in front of the other, running.

I thought, "She's going to fall flat on her face."

She whizzed past me straight to the house. She sat on the back porch step winded. Fortunately, I was struck dumb as she got up and ran back the way she came. She sat at the other end of the walk and panted.

I ran to get Barbara from inside the house. I was describing what had happened when there she came again, arms out, running back toward the house.

Shaking her head, Barbara said, "She's going to have a bloody nose before this is over with, Joan." Muttering to herself, she went back inside the house to finish up.

I was scared to watch too, but I was too fascinated not to. By the time the afternoon came to an end and parents began coming to get their children, I was used to Ana's running form. She hadn't fallen once. She kept on running, then resting, the whole afternoon. I didn't say a word to her, nor she to me. Her focus was totally on her running.

When she left for the day, I said, "Boy, I'll bet you're tired."

She smiled. "I'll be back tomorrow."

Ana ran for days. With kids, without kids, on the sidewalk, off the sidewalk, Ana never stopped running.

PART THREE

Stew Babies

31

"My Mom, My Dad, and My Lake Tahoe Will Beat You Up"

HE WAS THREE YEARS OLD. When he walked across the playroom his first day he stepped on a book, a toy, and Sara.

I said, "Mitchell, please don't step on people and toys. Step over or walk around."

He scrunched himself all up, clenched his fists, and screamed, "Don't tell me what to do. My mom and my dad and my brother and my Lake Tahoe will beat you up, you ugly fool you!" And he fell into a sobbing, inconsolable heap on the floor.

I went over to him.

"Get away from me and don't you touch me!" he cried. "My mom's coming!"

I sat down next to him and I said, "You know, I think you're really upset—"

"Don't you talk to me, you can't tell me what to do."

Believe me, I tried not to. I was astounded by his reaction. I thought to myself, Is this another Timmy D.? A verbal version, rather than a physical one?

But from the moment I met Mitch, my experience with him was very different. Rolph's memorable visit was a turning point for me because at that moment I *knew* I knew what I was doing. Prior to that visit, I had always assumed that someone, somewhere knew daycare better than I. That's why I went to Rolph in the first place—I wanted to consult with an expert. But when he came, I realized that I did know more about my daycare work than he did. However, even though I had more confidence, this did not take away my need or my search for excellent outside supervision.

It seemed impossible to sufficiently soften our discipline with this boy. Whenever we corrected him, he overreacted. When he threw three buckets full of sand out of the sandbox, I almost had to whisper, "I would like to suggest, Mitch, that we might try, as best we can, to keep the sand in the box so it doesn't become empty."

"Mind your own business, you dummy, or I'll punch you in the nose."

I was so taken aback at his responses that I almost laughed. But who could laugh at a little boy who barely belted all this out with veins bursting in a red face before he fell into helpless, wracking tears.

Well, you can imagine. I needed to talk with his parents. If I had learned nothing else from my experience with Timmy D. it was that parents are the first resource when things aren't going well. Perhaps they would know why he was acting this way and could direct us in our efforts to deal with it.

As we sat in the main playroom by the fire sipping coffee, I said, "I realize we're just getting to know Mitch since it's only his first week, but I don't think I'm approaching him the best way. Whenever I try to correct him about a very simple thing—like throwing sand out of the sandbox—he gets very upset and angry. I was wondering how I could do it in a way that he could hear?"

As Barbara and I talked to Helen and Charles, his parents, all of us quickly came to see that a lot of Mitch's acting out and stepping on toes was a result of being very frightened about not being with his mother. He no longer cried when she left, but we all felt his fears continued. He managed these feelings by picking on other kids and bursting into tears when he thought we were criticizing him. It made sense that the offensive tactics he took were his response to the insecurity he was experiencing.

With Helen and Charles's help, we began at the meeting to develop a special approach to disciplining Mitch. It was very clear to all of us how bright, verbal, and overly sensitive he was. Since our slightest disapproval shattered his tender self-esteem and since he felt intense anxiety about separating from his mother, it made our home feel like a very scary place for him.

We first began by voicing our approval of everything we could, commenting constantly, "Why, Mitch, you sure know how to push that truck." "You sure know how to run." Frankly, after a while it got a bit boring glancing around and trying to find something to compliment him about. "Oh, you really did step over that brick nicely, Mitch." Or, "You are very good at getting books out for yourself."

We didn't yet comment on putting them back. If we had to tell Joel not to push Ana, or tell Bramble not to hurt Sandy, our dog, we did so broadly if Mitch was nearby, hoping he would notice that it was necessary for us to instruct and that the other children accepted it naturally. We wanted him to know that he wasn't being singled out, that every child needs to be told what to do at some point.

If he did something that needed our comment, for instance, purposely running into someone, I would say, "It's really important that all of us take care that we don't run into each other. And, Mitch, I want you to know that no one can run into you either. We are all safe here. And I'm the one who's in charge of keeping things safe. And I think you're a wonderful person. I just don't want you to run through the house and knock people down."

"DON'T YOU TELL ME WHAT TO DO. I *HATE* YOU! I'M GOING TO TELL MY MOMMY." Then he'd fall down and stay in a snit for a long time. Finally, he'd stop crying and the basic incident would be over, but then he'd sit and pout. And the more anybody tried to get him out of it, the moodier he got. I attempted it once. "Mind your own business you dummy!" he retorted. But still the other children came over. "Gee, Mitch, do you want—" "No. Don't talk to me."

We learned to discipline Mitch only when it was absolutely necessary: when another child needed us for defense against him or when he was deliberately doing something he knew was not allowed. It became quite easy to tell when he was testing or pushing us for limits.

In the beginning Mitch was instructed by us five or six times a day. Each time he responded with bizarre anger and inconsolable sobs. Believe me, Barbara and I looked the other way whenever we possibly could.

Then one afternoon in Mitch's third week, we were all outside when he came to me and said, "You got mad at Joel when he knocked all the bikes over but when I knocked over the purple one you didn't yell at me." It was true. I had, without anger, asked Joel to please set them all upright, and he did.

I said, "You knocked the purple bike over and I didn't yell at you?"

"Yeah, why not?"

"Because when I tell you what to do you get mad at me and fall down and cry. It makes me think it's too hard for you when I tell you what to do, so I only tell you what to do when it's very important. I feel your hurt feelings are more important than the bike getting knocked down and not picked up."

He puffed out his striped T-shirt. "I'm more important than Joel."

"No, Mitch, you're not *more* important than Joel or *less* important. To me, you're *both* important."

"You sure are stupid," he said. "I know that." And he walked away.

32

Meredith's Spot

FROM HER VERY FIRST DAY, Meredith, with her long blond curly hair and her frilly pink T-shirts, shed huge tears when her mother left. She wiped them onto one of her mother's blouses which she clutched in her hands. It was an old one her mother had given her as a kind of security blanket.

Even though her morning separation from her mother continued to be painful, Meredith liked coming to daycare, enjoyed playing, and made friends easily; she quickly came to love us. But no matter how joyfully she spent the day, her morning partings with her mother remained the same. And although her mother was getting increasingly upset, for she didn't get to see the wonderful time her daughter was having, we knew how much she loved being with us and we were not concerned.

Then one morning, the tears stopped. Meredith didn't cry or pick up her mother's blouse when her mother walked out the front door. In fact, she barely noticed her going, so intent was she on joining her friends in the playroom. But all was not well. When her mother came to get her in the afternoon the tears came back in a torrent. Now she found it very painful to leave us.

When these tears continued for a number of weeks, we came up with a new idea. We asked Meredith if she would like to borrow something special overnight and return it the next morning. This transitional object, a doll, did not make her leavings any less tearful, but that doll from our house said: you are going to come back, see, you have to return me, and I'll be company for you until tomorrow.

Meanwhile, her parents reported various tearful good-byes—to the trash bag when the trash truck took it away, to the merry-go-round, "but it will miss me because I won't be here," and when replacing one telephone with another, "but can't we keep them both? That one will be so lonely without us."

"Meredith, please don't sit on the book. I can't read it if you do."

One of the hardest lessons for little Meredith when she first came was that she couldn't sit on top of the book that I was reading. We sit in a circle and sometimes I read to the children for two hours at a stretch. They come and go, sometimes looking at their own books or playing in different parts of the playroom. I value this time because it is one way that children learn to love reading and books. Besides, I love reading to them. Sometimes I stop and we discuss things along the way. But I couldn't do anything when Meredith sat in the middle of the book.

"Meredith, you can't sit on the book because we're looking at it. You can look at the book with us and sit on my lap." She looked up at me, scrunched up her little face, and burst into silent tears. This truly broke her heart.

Then she got up and walked around the room, knocking down toys that other children were playing with.

I looked at the children sitting around me and said, "I know it makes you angry when someone spoils your game but this is hard for Meredith. All of our attention is away from her and on the book. You know, we're all going to have to help Meredith. I can't promise how soon it will happen, but I can promise you one thing—she will grow up. And it will happen sooner if we're all patient with her."

Jennifer, by this time four, said, "Will she *really?*"

I admit at this point it was hard to believe.

The next day as I was reading, the same thing happened again, so I stopped and said, "I would like to ask all of us to ask Meredith to get off the book. Then we'll give her a chance to do it."

So all the children yelled, "Get off the book, Meredith!" Then they stared at her, waiting.

She looked around and then at me. The children and I looked back.

She looked down at her feet and said, "Meredith off the book," and got off the book just as if it were her own idea.

Over the weeks, we made the transition from "off the book" to "on Joanie's lap." It was difficult for me because I couldn't hold her for two hours. So one day, exasperated at myself for failing to subtly get her off, I said, once again in front of the other children, "Meredith, I really do want you to sit on the floor with the rest of the children."

"No," she said shaking her shiny curls. "Joanie's lap."

"Well, my lap gets tired. I can hold you for a little while, but not all the time."

Then Jennifer said, "Here's Meredith's spot!"

I looked over at her, gratefully. "Right," I smiled, knowing that if you name it, they believe it. "Meredith's Very Own Spot." And I gestured at the place Jennifer was pointing to. "There's your spot to sit on."

"No!" Meredith said petulantly, sticking her lower lip out. "Joanie's lap!"

"Well, when my lap gets tired, that's your spot." I looked around at the children. "Now nobody sit on Meredith's spot."

Jennifer sat next to that spot all morning and whenever someone new came in, she would say, "No, you can't sit here. It's Meredith's spot!"

The next morning, as usual, I was reading and a group of children were gathered around me when Meredith arrived and went right to my lap. I didn't say anything. But Jennifer was sitting by a vacant spot and every time someone tried to sit there, she'd shake her head and say, "You can't sit there. It's Meredith's."

About ten minutes went by and Meredith got down from my lap and sat on her spot.

I've learned that the more patient we are with the children the better able they are to use their own judgment. Meredith had time to do it herself, and using her own judgment as to when, developed trust in herself. And the more we allow the other children's support and help, the faster we get to what works for all of us.

The next day when I opened the book, there she was sitting on her spot, waiting for the story to begin.

33

The Monster of
the Playroom

EVERY THURSDAY, KATE THORTON, our play-drama teacher, came at ten. After warm-up—"Let's all be snakes . . . come on, that's it, let's slither around the floor. . . . Let's all be eensy weensy spiders, let's climb up those webs!"—she'd sit on the playroom rug, toss her lovely auburn hair, and ask, "Okay. What shall we play today?"

A lithe young woman, Kate had been a kindergarten teacher for a number of years. One day she finally said to herself, "I'm not teaching in public schools anymore, there must be another way," and she left to become Smiley the clown. When I met her, she had gotten tired of entertaining children and had been studying mime. Interested in myths and fairy tales, this became a vehicle to work again with children. Sensitive and inventive, she was the one who first noticed that Mitch could only be the bad guy in the children's plays. -

"The Three Little Pigs!" someone would invariably cry out in response to her question.

Kate, becoming the mother pig, says, "You pigs are big enough now. You need to go out into the world and make your own houses and live your own lives. As much as I'd like to have you here, it's time for you to move on." So all the children would have to go out and they would meet a man with straw and with him they would build a straw house, and they would meet a man with sticks and with him they would build a stick house. Then the industrious ones would get together and build the brick house. Then the wolf would come. The children loved to play this over and over. It was their way to grapple with fears of being alone in the world, without Mom and Dad. We must have done the three pigs almost every week for months.

Or some child would say, "Let's do a scary one."

A child would begin: "I was walking through the woods, and I was all by myself and then I got really scared and there was a wolf and he came out of the woods and he chased me and I ran all the way home."

Or Kate, becoming the child, would hear a noise. "What's that?"

"What?" the children would all say.

"What was that noise, Mommy, Daddy, Mommy-Daddy?"

There would always be plenty of children who'd rush in and be Mommies and Daddies: "What's the matter? What's the matter?" And plenty of children who would rush toward them, saying, "I heard this big noise and I'm so scared." The Mommies and Daddies would say, "Oh that? That's just the wind in the trees against the window. Go to sleep now, little children. Go back to sleep."

Sometimes Kate would have all the children act out one character in unison. This is when she discovered that Mitch could be a wonderful wolf, a frightening witch, a terrible troll.

"Let's be witches," she'd say. "Are witches scary?"

"Yes!" the children shouted.

"Let's make a scary face. Let's see those teeth. Let's hear those witchy sounds." The children would be as scary as they could, especially Mitch. Kate joined in with the children, doing all the actions with them. I sat on the sofa with Barbara where we'd catch the younger ones when they frightened themselves. Then we'd huddle there and watch the others at a safe distance.

"Okay, let's all be fairy godmothers. Oh, aren't we lovely. Look at my crown, look at my wand, aren't we beautiful and good?"

But Mitch would never act this part out.

"Oh, look, there's Cinderella, she's crying. She wants to go to the ball. But look, her clothing, oh no, she can't go in rags! Come bring your magic wands. Ah there, look how beautiful her dress is. Good-bye, Cinderella, have fun at the ball. Be back at 12:00 or *you know what.*"

"Yes, you dummy," Mitch would say, snapping his suspenders. "You sure are ugly in your rags. Your coach is now a pumpkin, you're so stupid."

Kate constantly challenged Mitch to play the good characters: Snow White, the Prince, fairy godmother, the good hunter, Red Riding Hood, the gentle monster. For it was the good, the warm, and the mushy that frightened him. We wanted to see what might happen if he played those parts. So Kate led him to play out parts that transformed evil to good and dark to light. But the part he liked best of all was the monster of the playroom.

In the deep, dark, slimy waters in the middle of our playroom floor wallowed Mitch the monster, all by himself.

Kate noticed him and said, "Oh, look at him. He's horrible!" Wallowing in the terrible dark deep, Mitch was rolling about, making terrible monster faces, noises, grunts, groans, and threatening gestures.

"Look out, don't go near the pool, children, or you may

fall in." As he listened to her, Mitch became beside himself with delight.

Ten children tiptoed around the pool as Mitch grabbed at their feet.

"Children," Kate said. "Do you think that monster wants to be so bad and ugly?" Children: "NO!" (Mitch: "YES!")

"Shall we help him to be good and happy?" Children: "YES!" (Mitch: "NO!")

"Do you think he wants to get out of that cold and slimy water?" Children: "YES!" (Mitch: "NO!")

"Come on, monster, it must be cold and dark and fearful in there. Don't you want to come out and play with us?" (Mitch: "NO!")

"We like you. Here—we'll sprinkle magic powder to transform you. Children, do you have your magic powder?" Children: "YES!"

"Come on, then. Here we come, monster. We will help you. We want you to come with us." And Kate and the children began to move toward him.

Mitch stood up and said, "I'm not playing anymore. You guys sure are dumb."

34

I Save a Life

URING THIS TIME, SANDY, our beloved golden retriever, was pregnant. And one day during school, she began having her second litter upstairs in a large wooden box. I allowed the children to come and go, watching her. Sandy was always so happy to see each child that even as she worked at having her puppies, she wagged her behind in greeting!

Several parents came to pick up their children and stayed until eight or so when the last pup of a litter of ten was born. As each one came out, she licked them. Her rough, warm tongue not only cleaned each one but stimulated it enough so it could gasp out its first breaths.

But one puppy couldn't breathe. Sandy pushed it toward her nipples with her nose, licking it continually, but it just lay there, very still. Since she was already panting, the next one on the way—she had had six by now—she finally gave up and left the still pup alone to give her full attention to the seventh.

I got a rough washcloth and continued rubbing the still pup. But as I rubbed, I realized that this lifeless little puppy was actually full of mucus—in its nose, and in its mouth when I forced it open. I quickly picked it up, and using the washcloth because the pup was very slippery, I held it by the tail and swung it in circles above my head. I had read about this technique in a dog book before Sandy's first litter.

The mucus came flying out and I stopped and roughed the pup up with the washcloth, quickly wiping away whatever was in its nostrils and mouth. Then I picked it up again and holding its tail with the cloth, I swung it over my head. Soon enough the little pup began to breathe. I gave it to Sandy because it felt cold. Exchanging pups with her, I began rubbing the next one with my washcloth. And as I watched, Sandy pushed the little one I had been swinging toward her nipple and it hungrily began to nurse.

A few weeks later, Meredith was eating an apple. She always ate by stuffing her mouth as fully as she could and swallowing part of what she chewed as she continued to stuff more into her already full mouth. Mealtimes with her were always noisy because she couldn't breathe very well through her nose. So whenever I watched her eat, I found myself holding my breath like she did to chew and swallow and then afterward, catching up with my own breathing.

This particular chilly fall morning, the children were not only having hot chocolate and toast but eating apples peeled and cut up. Meredith, as usual, was stuffing herself. Then Joel dropped his cup of chocolate, surprising her, and Meredith suddenly inhaled a piece of apple which lodged deep in her throat.

This was very different from the way a child usually chokes, for Meredith made no noise. Her eyes and mouth became wide open, her face turning blue.

I reached out and grabbed her, turning her upside down.

Nothing.

I beat her on the back.

Nothing.

Then I remembered that little puppy of Sandy's and I grabbed her by her ankles, and holding her upside down, began to swing her in semicircles, back and forth. A piece of apple the size of a Ping-Pong ball flew out and hit the window above the sink. She began coughing and gasping and, thank heavens, breathing!

It was a horrible experience for me. Meredith was well into her second cup of hot chocolate—no more apple, please—while I still sat trembling next to her, trying to recover from what I knew was certain death, except for a bit of luck.

Later, another doctor friend, Dr. Marc, commented that I could have broken Meredith's neck. Wide-eyed, I asked, "What should I have done?"

He started telling me about a long needle inserted just so into the windpipe, just above the bone which was located at the base of the neck where . . .

"Don't you think that's just a bit impossible for me to do?" I finally said.

Today we know the Heimlich maneuver and have instructions in what to do about an obstructed airway. But, thank heavens, we haven't had another incident like that. Yet.

35

Mitch & Sara,
a Love Story

Look out, MITCH, YOU'RE IN MY WAY."

"You look out, you fool, you hit me with the broom."

Sara and Mitch were cleaning sand off the back porch with broom, shovel, and pail. It was late fall so there was a curious mix of sand and beautiful plum leaves that had fallen everywhere.

"You have to get out of my way, Mitch. I'll never get this mess cleaned up."

"You sure won't. You don't know how to do anything."

"You sweep then. I'm not going to help."

Mitch took the broom and said, "You have to help. Joanie and Barbara said we have to clean up. You are so dumb, Sara. If you don't work, I'm going to tell."

"*I'm* going to tell. You are mean to me and make me unhappy." She ran to Barbara. "Barbara, Mitch is being mean

to me again." By this time Sara was in tears so Barbara picked
her up.

Mitch said, "Okay, Sara doesn't have to clean up, so I'm
sure not going to, right, Sara?"

Sara peeked over Barbara's shoulder and, obviously feeling not so bad after all, put her head up and said, "Right,
Mitch. We don't have to do *everything*."

"You feel like it's too much to do?" Barbara asked, looking at them both.

"Yes, we aren't going to finish."

"I'll help," Barbara said. "Mitch, you shovel up the big
pile of sand and put it in the pails. Sara can empty the pails
into the sandbox and I'll sweep too and keep the piles coming." She smiled at them. "Sometimes a job is too big for two
people."

"Right, Mitch, it's too big just for two workers, Barbara
will help us."

"Right, Sara, cause you don't know how to sweep."

"You don't either, dum-dum."

"Well, I can sweep better than you, you fool," and so
it continued until the sand and leaves were all cleaned up.

Sara and Mitch were best friends/best enemies for the
first six months they were here together. Bickering and bat-
tling, they snorted and sniveled, putting each other down and
picking each other up.

They reminded all of us of a little old couple who had
lived together for too long. It was almost too much to hope
that either would ever opt for another relationship since their
play was exclusive. When they allowed another child to join
in, their tight partnership still remained constant.

If a bucolic tranquillity had been our daycare's fondest
goal, we would have spent all our time trying to separate
Mitch and Sara. And I feel we would have done them a dis-
service. The volcanic outward appearance of their relationship belied the real need they had for each other. So we didn't

try to change the nature of their partnership; rather, we merely assisted its day-to-day workings whenever necessary.

One lunchtime Sara got a stool, whereas Mitch didn't, as three other children were already sitting on them. Stools had become the favorite place for the children recently. In our kitchen there are four stools at one small square table, and four benches at the other, larger one. Since at least six children always wanted to sit on the stools, it was a race. Usually if both Mitch and Sara didn't get a stool, they sat together on a bench at the larger table, neither taking the only stool that was left.

So Mitch said to Sara, "Get off that stool."

Sara retorted, "No, I am not going to 'cause you will get it then."

"No, I won't," Mitch said emphatically.

"You might."

"Mitch," I said from where I was standing by the stove, "do you want Sara to sit at the other table with you?"

Mitch said, "Yes."

Sara said, "I don't want to sit at that table. I want a stool."

As I stirred the macaroni and cheese, I said, "Okay, Mitch, Sara doesn't want to give up the stool."

Mitch said to Sara, "You better get off that stool or I won't be your best friend." This was a threat that they both used dozens of times a day. He then took a swipe at her head but she backed out of his range just in time. She still didn't move from the stool so Mitch tried to tip it over. Sara shrieked, and I said, "Cut it out, Mitch. Sara can keep the stool and you had better find a place for yourself right now."

He immediately left the kitchen, going straight into the playroom. Sara continued to sit on her stool but she began to get nervous. "Why isn't Mitch having his lunch?" she finally asked as I served the other children, asking each what they wanted.

"He wants a stool," I said. "He'll get over it soon and come in."

"He said he wouldn't be my friend if I don't give him the stool."

"He always says that, Sara. Eat your lunch."

But Sara was upset. She got down from her stool and went into the playroom. Barbara followed them far enough down the hall to hear Sara say, "You can have the stool, Mitch. I'll sit on the bench."

"It's too late now, Sara," he said. "You should have given me the stool when I told you to."

"But I wanted the stool."

"Well, you've got it, so go sit on it, stupid."

At this point, Barbara came back into the kitchen and called Sara back to her lunch. Sara came back and said, "Wait a minute, I'll be right back." But she didn't come back. This time Barbara didn't follow her.

Soon enough she came back in the kitchen and with furious eyes glared at me, saying, "Joanie, it's all your fault."

I looked up as I sprinkled Parmesan cheese on Todd's macaroni. "What is all my fault?"

"You shouldn't have gotten mad at Mitch about the stool."

"What?" I said, turning from the table. "He slapped you and then he tried to push the stool out from under you."

"I know," she said, pouting. "But it is all your fault." And with that she ran back into the playroom.

This time I followed. There Mitch was, feeling sorry for himself on the pillows. It was still hard for him to take any correction from me. Sara sat nearby, comforting him. I looked at both of them and said, "Are you two coming for lunch?"

Mitch looked up. "No, we decided that if we don't eat lunch anymore then we won't fight about stools, right, Sara?"

Sara looked up at me with the daggers still in her eyes. "Right, Mitch," she said.

"Sounds like a good solution," I said. "As long as you don't get hungry," and I walked back to the kitchen.

A few minutes later Mitch and Sara came to the bench and had lunch. As they sat down Mitch said, "You are right, Joanie, it was a good solution, we both got hungry."

36

Dan

HE STOOD AT THE WINDOW waiting for his mother for what must have seemed like a lifetime. He was $2\frac{1}{2}$.

It rained, the sun came out, children came, went, still he stood by the window. I sat down beside him and opened a book, but I could not lure him away.

The simplest incident started it. His mother, Norma, handed me his medicine when she brought him that morning. It was a typical decongestant that children often take when they're getting a cold. She said, "Daniel doesn't like to take medicine from me."

I said, "Of course not, you're his mother."

"If it's okay with Daniel, could you give him a teaspoon of this? If it's not okay with him, then don't."

At that instant he threw himself at her, screaming, twisting, and tearing, beating her with his fists. But she was very calm, and said, in the midst of the pummeling, "Daniel, you don't have to take the medicine. I already told Joan that. Look, I'll take it home with me."

She was wearing a silk suit and she got down on her knees as she grabbed his fists. His face was red and full of tears. And nothing she said made one bit of difference in his behavior.

Finally, she gave up. "I've got to go."

"Okay," I said, and I pried Daniel off her as she went out the door.

He ran after her as the door shut in his face. He ran over to the panel of little windows by the door and screamed, pounding on the glass with his hands. She turned, waved, and hurried down the steps, shutting the little gate to the deck behind her.

This kind of separation was not unusual for a child; it was no different at this point than Meredith's or Mitch's. Yet.

I left him at the window to calm down and went into the large playroom, sat down at my place by the fire, and began reading aloud to the usual group of children who gathered around me. Meredith found her spot, Mitch got out three books and couldn't decide which one to have me read, while Ana kept on playing with her friends Sally and Bramble. At one point, Barbara came in from the kitchen where she was making breakfast and saw him still at the window. "Danny," she said. "Want to help me with breakfast?"

His little hand tightened into a fist as it lay against the windowpane. He did not move or acknowledge her presence. I smelled blueberry muffins and scrambled eggs. When Barbara called the children for breakfast, I set the book aside and went into the hallway. "Come on, Danny, breakfast, blueberry muffins, yummmmm." But he did not move.

It was an overcast day. Sandy walked up to him and rubbed her back against Danny's sturdy bare legs. I had made a good roaring fire, and I was afraid he'd get cold with only shorts on and a T-shirt so I got out a sweater and went toward him—but he took his hand off the window only briefly enough to shove the sweater, and me, away.

Later, I sat down beside him by the window with a puzzle and started to play it. "Look, Danny, I have—" for almost always a child can be seduced by an amazing puzzle. But not Dan. Not this morning. He never even turned around.

It was then that I noticed the moisture running down his legs. I said nothing. But for a little boy like Danny, used to the toilet, to wet his pants is as ignominious as it is for an adult. But he would not leave that window even for a moment.

I called his mother at her office but she was in court. Her assistant said Mrs. MacFarlande would be here as soon as she could.

Children flew by Danny, in and out the two doors leading from one playroom to the other. Books were dropped behind him, toys. He did not move or glance around. Barbara called him for lunch. I knew he must be very hungry. But still he would not come.

Two of my own grown children came through the door, the mailman put mail in the slot, it fell unnoticed at his feet. The day darkened outside, it sprinkled, then the sun came out, and still Danny did not budge.

Finally, just before naptime, I glanced out the big playroom window and saw his mother hurrying up the front steps.

And the moment she opened the door he threw himself at her, screaming and kicking—exactly the place where he left off. She caught him by the arm.

"Well, Joan," she said. "I'll see you tomorrow." And she went out the front door.

I walked to the window and stared after them. Here was a little boy who up until now had been a perfect gentleman— quiet, benign, biding his time until his mom came back. And now he was screaming, pulling at her all because she wanted him to take his cold medicine. I shook my head. I didn't get it. Here was his mother, in the midst of it all, calmly opening the little deck gate with one hand, and without visibly changing her expression, carrying this screaming little banshee out to her car.

I thought, "This is very strange. Something is definitely the matter."

37

The Little Boy
Who Never Got
Enough

I T STARTED VERY NORMALLY. Norma sat across from Barbara and me, drinking coffee. Frank, Daniel's father, sat next to her. They were listening to my concerns about their son.

They hadn't brought Daniel to the conference. This was unusual as I ask parents to bring their child. It is never "we" against "him" or "her," or that we try to keep anything from the child. Children know everything that we know and it is comforting to hear it said. But this conference . . . it turned out to be a good thing Danny didn't come. . . .

I was telling them how disconcerted I was by what happened with Dan over the cold medicine. It seemed so out of character with the Daniel that I had come to know in the last six months. I told them that I found him a sweet, tentative boy, just sort of waiting out his time until she came back each day.

Then Norma asked me to tell her husband Frank what

had gone on that morning. I told him quite honestly that in all my years providing daycare, I had not seen a little child hold on to his rage for so long. He had kept it, a slow burn at the window, for three hours. He had even wet his pants.

Frank didn't respond. He sat back into the sofa as I was talking to him, his eyes half closed as he listened. His wife seemed distracted.

Summing up, I said, "It just seemed out of character. All that anger. I was surprised."

There was silence. I sat there across from them in my easy chair. Barbara was sitting next to me on the floor, drinking a Pepsi. And I was beginning to wonder if we were all thinking about the same incident. I couldn't understand why we weren't having a discussion about it. I knew them to be kind and loving people who were dedicated parents but they didn't seem to be here with me. I finally looked over and said, "Am I saying anything you don't know?" I didn't think so because parents always know more than I do about their child.

More silence.

I cleared my throat, trying again. "I mean, is this a surprise? Am I describing another child to you? Is this the Daniel you know?" I asked, smiling a bit.

Norma shook her head. "That's not it," she said quietly.

There was a long silence. Barbara coughed. I looked at them. "This must be very hard for you . . ."

Frank leaned forward. He looked at me directly and said, "This kid has been sullen and moody from the day he was born. This kid rules our household!"

Then Norma leaned toward Barbara and me and said, "He cries all the time! We don't feel we can do anything right! And we can't figure out what we did wrong. Lisa, his older sister, is just fine." Her eyes filled with tears. "My pain is about having such an unhappy child. I keep feeling that it lies within me. If I were different then he would be different, happier, instead of so moody. We don't know from one day to the next what mood he'll be in. When we realized, as a baby, that he was so unhappy I took a leave from my law practice. But nothing I was able to do made things better for him. I became very frustrated and then disappointed in myself as my leave was almost up and he was getting even more difficult. The worst for me was that since Lisa was doing well, why wasn't Daniel? We hadn't done anything different with him. I went back to work, worse off than I was before, for now I didn't know what possibly could comfort him."

I watched her strained face as she talked and I felt the despair she felt when she didn't know what to do for him. She told us that as Daniel got older he became harder to deal with. They weren't able to do any of those family things others were able to do.

"One time, *one time*, we took a family trip—how long ago was it, Norma?—a year and a half ago?" Frank asked. "Danny cried from the moment he got into the car until two hours later when I turned around and headed for home. I couldn't stand it! He was upset about a fly in the car, I don't remember what it was really, but we knew it was over. If Daniel didn't want to go, he was capable of crying the whole weekend."

Norma added, "I feel very badly for Daniel. I wish it could have been different for him. I wish it were different now. We aren't enough for him and I don't know what would be enough." She sighed and then said, "What you saw him do, Joan, over the decongestant, is for us an everyday experience."

I didn't know what to say. I was so surprised by their account of his behavior. It was so unlike my experience of him that now I felt like I didn't know him at all. My first organized thought was to wonder at the rage this little boy must be sitting on if he's so quiet and well mannered here and volatile at home.

I glanced from Frank's anxious face to Norma's tear-stained one and asked, "Has he been worse at home since he's started daycare? It takes a big effort to be well behaved for a whole day."

"Frankly, Joan," Norma replied, "there's really no such thing as worse."

I looked over at both she and Frank, and I said, "I just had no idea." I hesitated, not sure where to begin. "I just don't think it's healthy for Daniel to continue along with us, holding back his feelings in the hours he spends with us."

"Yes," Norma said.

"You understand that right now we can only have a superficial relationship with him. This also explains his aloofness with the other kids. He appears not to really care about what they do or say. I don't think," I shook my head, "that he can be really a part of what goes on here if he's so caught up with what's not right in general for him."

Frank sat forward on the sofa, listening intently.

"At the same time," I went on, "I'm not sure that even if we were able to get him to unleash some of these feelings that we could really handle them." As I spoke, I knew I wanted Daniel to stay with us. I smiled. "I suppose it's up to the four of us to figure this out. Do you have any ideas?"

"Us?" Frank asked.

Norma shook her head. "I don't think so."

I hadn't a clue either. But I knew who would.

After my experience with Rolph, I was a bit cautious about having another supervisor in my life. I read everything I could get my hands on about early child development, education, and play therapy. I read Piaget, Anna Freud, Fraiberg, and Erikson. I visited other daycares and knew I was doing it as well or better than anyone. But I wanted to know more and be increasingly effective. I began to feel that I had gone about as far as I could on my own.

What I had always known instinctively was that every daycare provider needs supervision—that is, someone they can go to when they have problems with a child that they can't solve alone. So when Carol called me and said, "I want you to come and meet Dr. Dru, he's this little gnome of a man from England, kind of ageless, Joan. I can't put my finger on it, but I *know* he is just magic with kids. Let me introduce you," I was ready.

I met him at Carol's birthday party for Tina. Dru gave her a picture of a beautiful white unicorn. I've never forgotten the image because that's exactly how Dru seemed to me—like a unicorn, one of a kind, special. Here was a child psychologist I could talk to.

Since that time Dr. Dru has become a tremendous resource for Barbara and me. We have an art resource, a music one, legal, health care advice, speech therapy, and Dru is one of the most valuable persons we have. I always know that whatever I find when I observe a child closely we can do something about.

In the kitchen I thought about my unique position with parents. I was neither parent nor child, but could empathize with both points of view. Nor was I a therapist. But as an outside observer, ardently interested in Daniel's welfare, I could be very helpful to them, *if* I could do it in a way that both could accept.

Barbara and I had learned to make a referral to Dr. Dru in a way that worked. It was never done hurriedly and without trying everything else first. Parents are always willing to guide us in our efforts to make a difference with their troubled child. Yet to recommend professional intervention at this moment to Frank and Norma could feel to them like a sudden and impulsive move.

As I returned to the playroom, I saw the shadows of the bright fire hit and glance off the walls. Barbara had stirred it up while I was gone. I smiled at Daniel's parents, preparing to cram months of work into a few moments.

I began by explaining that each of their children had a different view of reality. "For Lisa, your lives made sense. She adapted and grew without incident. For Danny, I imagine that something about his early experience was difficult for him. But how could you know what that is? When you realized how difficult it was for him, Norma, you left work and tried to give him what he needed." She nodded. "I don't know what else you could have done. Now it's two years later. And from what you're telling me it seems that he's still suffering from some experience of his infancy."

I continued. "Danny's been with us awhile now. If he were free of these upsetting feelings that he can't manage, he would not be so tentative but be involved and active in this world." I swallowed. "It seems to me that we've come to a point where we can say Daniel needs something more."

"What do you mean, something more?" Norma asked.

"Psychological help. I don't know your thoughts about therapy for young children, but I've seen that it can make all the difference in the world. The therapy I recommend allows parents to see that the troubles they need help with belong to the child. Some kids seem to get stuck and no matter what their parents do they can't seem to move on. You know," I smiled, "Lisa and Daniel both had the same experience, and Daniel didn't do well. Same parents, same situation. What was different for Daniel is still with him and has become a barrier he can't break through, do you see?"

They were both listening intently and nodded. They wanted to believe it wasn't their fault and that Daniel's behavior could change.

Frank chewed his lip. "If we make the decision to send Danny to therapy, what will happen to him there?"

"Yes," Norma said. "How would a therapist work with Daniel? I don't think he has the words, you know, he's so young."

I told them that Dr. Dru, the child therapist I work with, has toys and a sand tray with hundreds of miniatures—people, trees, houses—all the things that Danny would find in real life. And also, every monster imaginable that he might find in his fantasies. I explained that Daniel would be encouraged to play with the miniatures, placing them in the sand tray and that as time went by he would make his environment in the sand. Dru, using this sand play and a family history, and his therapeutic skills, would be able to find out just what it was that really caused Daniel difficulty. I told them that Dr. Dru describes this trauma or surprise in a child as a tiny bump on a reel of tape. Every child goes through some trauma or surprise. It can be a stay in the hospital, a fire, a scare of some sort. We can never know how it will affect them. Why is it that Toby had appendicitis as a child with no adverse reaction, whereas Lorna had a cast on her foot and this influenced her development tremendously. These are the little bumps we're talking about. And no matter how much tape you put on top of it, you're always going to have that little bump. That's the bump that therapy is going to smooth out.

Since they were clearly at their wits' end, both of them agreed it would be good for Danny to go. When they left that night Norma had Dru's number in her purse.

After they left, I asked Barbara, "How long do you think it will take them to call him?"

Sometimes just having the therapist's telephone number in the purse can offer enough hope to keep a parent going for months.

38

A Baby Changes Everything in Your Life

LATER, AS I GOT READY FOR BED, I sat down in my easy chair and thought about Frank and Norma and parenting.

For myself, I thought I knew everything about parenting by the time my first son John was born. I had taken care of both my sisters since I was sixteen, and I was sure I could care for my own just as efficiently.

But when I gave birth to John something happened.

What I felt was indescribable. He was *mine*. This was *my* baby. And I leaned down and I rested my forehead against his, letting myself take him in for the first time. And I became frightened. Who I was was not enough to raise this baby. I didn't know enough. And I realized for the first time how vulnerable we both were. What if I died before he grew up?

Prior to having him, I used to be very reckless—reckless with a guardian angel. I drove too fast, I swam too far out; all of that would stop now that he was born.

My friend Carol says that she wouldn't walk across the street except in a crosswalk after her daughter Tina was born.

My son John grew up and became a winner. I don't know how many games of cards he's lost to me but he still feels that he's never lost a game of Rook. His reality, in my opinion, is so askew in his favor that at times it is insufferable. But when his son, Michael John, was born, he went through the same transformation that I did. He said to me late one night, "Mom, for the first time in my life I feel vulnerable." And he wiped the tears from his eyes. "I can't believe it. I hate feeling this frightened."

Right along with the protective urge that is awakened in parents are the feelings of inadequacy. All the ways that you and I were vulnerable when we were little and that we worked so hard to overcome and that we have all these trophies to show for don't make one whit of difference when we have a child.

The child comes with his or her own agenda. And their agenda, as it unfolds, changes us. Danny's parents are an excellent example. I sat with them, two lawyers, absolutely lucid and intelligent, who had adapted to the quirks of their son's personality. Before speaking to us, they were so full of guilt and powerlessness, thinking that *they* had caused it all. Consequently, they couldn't begin to see how much this little being simply by his birth and by virtue of his unique personality had rearranged their entire lives. They didn't go on vacations, they didn't go out to dinner as a family; in fact, they couldn't leave home happily at all—all because who Daniel was had changed their lives. Indeed, their lives had been reduced to work and Danny.

They had prepared for the baby, of course, but they had no idea to what extent, when each child comes into the world, he or she changes the environment that they come into. And even though they already had one child, they were totally unprepared for how each is so completely different from the other.

And it seemed to me, as I sat there that night, that it was

true, Daniel was an extreme case. But nonetheless, here were two parents who were very smart in the world and even counseled other people and yet had no idea how powerless they had gotten around their own child.

It all amazes me, really. A baby comes into the world, $7\frac{1}{2}$ pounds, about the size of a large trout, and it changes the way we do everything in our lives. Whether we lock our doors, or wear our seat belts or pay our bills on time or not, we are now vulnerable. A baby changes everything in our lives.

39

Stew Babies

"JOAN, IS IT TRUE? Does Kate really cook dolls here?" a nervous parent asked me one morning.

"No," I said, smiling. "Kate would never do anything like that, it's the children who do."

It all began with a little boy named Terry who loved to crash. He'd get in one of the toy cars and run straight into the garage, smacking it so hard that the car would actually go partway up the garage door.

Terry's stories, during play-drama, were always about huge catastrophes. The children loved to act them out because they love disasters. Terry would get a doll from the shelf and say, "The baby's sick, the baby's sick," and then he would run into the dining room and stuff the doll out the window saying, "The baby's sick, the baby's sick," as it fell outside. Kate would say, "Let's go get the baby," and all the

158

children would run down the front steps, swerve around the side of the house, and rescue the doll. Terry would wear a stethoscope as he threw the doll out the window, or when he did his emergency medical work, calling in nurses and doctors and everybody. He did all this with great fervor. It wasn't sad to him at all, or to any other child. It was *exciting*.

Then one day when the children had gotten all the baby dolls together to play emergency, Terry started brutalizing one of them.

Kate watched for a moment and said, "Oh, this baby is crying."

In response, Terry slapped the doll, saying, "Stop crying, baby."

Kate said, "Well, I think the baby has stopped crying."

"No, she hasn't," Terry said. *Whack.* "Stop crying, baby."

Then Jennifer joined him, saying, "We're going to stick her in this pot of water." The baby went into the pot of water. Then Sara said, "Look, we're cooking the baby!" And Mitch added, "Good idea, let's eat her!" So that's how they started playing Stew Babies. This lasted for another six months.

Every time Kate came they'd get all the babies out and put them in a pot of boiling water to cook them.

"Now, let's eat one."

Kate, always going along, would say, "Oh, yum yum yum, she sure is good."

"Yeh, yum yum yum."

"This is a good baby," Mitch would say, smacking his lips as well as his suspenders.

"This one is *my* baby," Meredith would say, picking another one out. "Yum yum yum."

After a while, though, some of the parents got a little concerned when their children came home and said, "We ate babies today. We hit the baby. We put her in boiling water and then we ate her. Yum yum yum. It was a *good* baby."

But I wasn't concerned. It felt benign, even a little boring, as I sat through so many of these hours.

I know some "experts" say not to read children scary books. The theory is that children have nightmares and are frightened of things, so we need to stop scaring them with frightening stories. Yet Bruno Bettelheim, the great child psychologist, explained in his book on fairy tales why they are so important and necessary in a child's life. Whatever is written there will not create monsters. These are already in children's minds. Rather, a good fairy tale gives children words, ideas, and the possibility of communicating about the monsters already lurking inside.

And, also, of course, children's media itself is all about monsters. If you look at "Sesame Street," the characters are all monsters. *There's a Monster Under My Bed, Where the Wild Things Are*—there are tons of books about being frightened. It's not that we're giving children fears with these books and this kind of television. What we're doing is giving our impression of those fears because we were all children once. I can still work myself into a frenzy that there're monsters around. For me, of course, they're not cookie monsters or dinosaurs but more about debt and disaster. Life is very frightening for children and they are at risk in the world. They're at risk to infantile disease. They're at risk to parents' moods. Until they are six or seven, they don't even possess the intellectual equipment to figure out why things happen. All they have is their feelings and their impression of things. Children this age experience the world differently from us. I just want to add, yes, and it's bizarre!

So when the children went home and told their parents, "We ate babies today. Yum yum yum. They were *good* babies!" and the parents came to me worried, I let them know that I thought what the children were doing was just fine.

They were exploring a monster or two.

40

Little Billy Goat Gruff

THURSDAY MORNING AND MITCH was on his way from the smaller playroom into the larger one. Sara was in the doorway and he pushed her over to get by. Sara began to cry.

Mitch put both his hands on his hips, and said, bending down to her, putting his nose to her nose, "How many times have I told you not to cry when I do stuff to you, Sara?" Then he walked into the playroom and sat down beside Kate, the play-drama teacher, who was about to begin.

Sara stopped crying, got up, and followed him. She tapped him on the shoulder, and as he turned she said, with her hands on her hips, leaning over him, "Well, then, when you are going to do stuff, you tell me first so I won't cry!" Then she sat down beside him.

"Well! What story should we do today?" Kate asked.

"Cinderella!" Next to Stew Babies, it was the children's

current favorite. We had been doing it off and on now for about two months.

Whenever Sara had a chance to choose what she wanted to be, it was always Cinderella. She knew that the stepsisters and the mother were going to be really mean to her, and that she would cry as she brushed the floor. The stepsister would come over to her as she scrubbed and say, "Scrub that floor!"

"I *am* scrubbing . . ."

"Well, do it harder!" They were supposed to be very cruel to her and make her life miserable.

I looked at Kate and said, "Sara's really crying."

"I know," Kate said. Then she touched Sara's arm, saying, "Okay, Cinderella, what can you say to that stepsister?"

"I don't know."

"Why don't you tell her, 'You scrub the floor. I'm not doing it anymore.' " But Sara couldn't do it. She'd start to say it, but would wind up repeating, "I'm scrubbing, I'm scrubbing."

I said, "Do you really want them to holler and yell at you like that, Sara?"

"I want to be Cinderella," she said emphatically. She really wanted to get to be Cinderella with the glass slipper, but first she had to get past the mean stepsisters.

Finally, one day, she chose it. "You scrub the floor, you old steps," she said. "I'm through."

"Children, do you have the magic powder?" Children: "YES!"

"Come on, then. Here we come, monster. We'll sprinkle magic powder to transform you." Kate and the children sprinkled the magic dust over Mitch. Succumbing to it, he slowly became limp in the pool.

"Are you dead, monster?"

A headshake, no.

"Do you want us to save you? We can, you know."

A less emphatic no.

"Let's go get him, good fairies. Let's hold him in our arms and give him all our love and magic. Shall we come, monster?"

Monster's head shakes no.

Finally, the other children began to get bored with all this waiting for Mitch to come out of the pool. At first, as always, it was fun to seduce him—trying this, trying that to get him to come out—for usually one child's good time is a lot of fun for the others.

But one day, Kate said, "We *can* change you, you don't have to be stuck there. Remember? We have the magic dust."

"Oh no, you can't change me, I'm too awful," Mitch said, resisting and resisting and just loving every minute of it, terribly nurtured by all the attention.

After twenty minutes or so of this, as Kate kept on saying, "Come on, Mitch," more and more of the children began walking away and finding something else to do. But she stayed with it until it could come to some conclusion from Mitch's point of view.

He kept resisting, saying, "No, leave me alone," and wallowing in his dark pool until Sally got so bored she said, "Let's go, you guys, I think he's dead."

When the group's attention was elsewhere, I'd notice Mitch pick up one of our magic wands and wave it a bit. Then he'd look around and stop. And he began to play some of the lesser hero parts in plays, as in "Three Billy Goats Gruff."

As the story goes, there's a troll underneath a bridge who threatens to eat anyone who crosses. A little billy goat goes across. The troll stops him, saying, "Who goes there? I am going to eat you up." The little billy goat says, "Oh, you don't want me—I'm too small. But my brother is coming and he's much bigger. He's perfect for you." "Great!" says the troll and he lets the little billy goat pass. Then the middle-sized one comes and passes it on to his brother, who's a giant billy goat. And when the biggest billy goat comes, he, of course, is big enough to smash the troll's body and bones.

Instead of always being the big goat, Mitch asked to be

the little one. But as he reached the top of the playroom slide that we used as a bridge, he couldn't cross over; instead, he'd become the bigger powerful goat who smashed the troll under the bridge to bits. No matter how he tried to be the little goat, this transformation occurred every time. Sometimes the group, like Sally, became impatient with his messing up the play, but more often than not, they were enchanted by the spontaneous turn of events.

At some point, Mitch stopped joining in at all. He played Play-Doh or puzzles in the kitchen with Danny, who continued to avoid most of the group play activities.

Kate would find him in the kitchen to say a few words but she never invited him to play. Other than, "Are you joining us?" Mitch: "NO." "Okay, I'll be in to say good-bye." She always sought him out before she left. While there was a goal in mind with Mitch to keep developing his other side, she was able to not have a goal for him to join in. Kate and I both saw this time out as progress. We knew that only he could give us the direction he needed to take. And soon enough, that direction came.

41

Mitch the Mouth

WITH A TWINKLE IN HIS EYE Mitch would say to me, "I hate you." I'd retort, "You do, eh? Oh, I love you." During the time when he was taking his hiatus from Kate, Barbara and I bantered with him, letting him have another way to let off steam. One reason we became sparring partners for his verbal insults was because his sense of humor was beginning to blossom.

"Well, I hate you both," and he would walk off laughing.

One day, when he said yet again, "Joanie, I hate you!" I put both my hands on my hips and I said, "Well, Mitch, I hate you too! Besides that I hated you the first day I laid eyes on you, you fink."

He looked at me, shocked at first, saw my expression, and then burst out laughing. He was $3\frac{1}{2}$.

He would say, "I hate you," and then, "You know I love you."

I'd say, "Love and hate, love and hate. You hate me and you love me all at the same time." Then the next day he would, with pesky humor, call me lizard lips, tell me to jump in the lake, and offer me a knuckle sandwich or a fat lip.

But unfortunately, during this time he was also insulting parents, without humor, in their comings and goings.

To Jennifer's mother, regarding her new haircut: "Your hair sure looks dumb."

To Sara's father: "Sara sure is stupid, don't you know that?" And to another father: "Why don't you go now, dum-dum? You're not staying here all day, are you?"

And he got into a couple of scrapes away from our place too. It seems he and his mother were in a Berkeley park frequented by families as well as a few older hippies. Mitch went over to a thirty-year-old man with lots of unkempt hair sitting under a tree and told him, "You sure are dirty."

The man was insulted by this and threatened Mitch with, "You better beat it, buster, if you know what's good for you."

Mitch immediately retorted, "Don't tell me what to do, you creep." At which point the fellow raised his hand to him just as Mitch's mom came on the scene.

She told the fellow, "You must be pretty down to let a $3\frac{1}{2}$-year-old get to you."

He looked up at her sheepishly.

Mitch quickly left the park with his mother, clearly shaken by what had happened.

About a week later, Mitch was over at the house of his three-year-old neighbor, Bethie. They were arguing about the rules for a card game when Mitch hit her. Knowing him, it was probably not much of a blow. As verbally abusive as Mitch truly was, he rarely lashed out physically. Bethie responded by biting him on the mouth.

Later, when Barbara and I heard about this, we laughed,

realizing that if we were to bite him, that's exactly where we'd do it too!

Hearing Mitch's cries, Bethie's mother arrived to intervene. Bethie said, "He hit me." "Well, what did you do?" her mother asked, when Mitch interrupted her, "You better get out of here." Shocked, Bethie's mother responded, "You've got it all wrong, Mitch." And she and her husband proceeded to lead him out of their house, saying, "Don't ever come back again."

This experience was frightening to Mitch. He didn't sleep well after that. His mother finally suggested to him that he might feel better if perhaps he'd tell me about it.

The next day was a glistening fall one, light and airy, the kind when the children seem to be delighted all day, except for Mitch. Late in the afternoon, while we were outside, he said, in response to my question about the incident in the park, "The man got mad, Joanie, and was going to hit me. My mom told me he was just a bad guy and not to talk to strangers. And boy was he strange!"

I asked, "What happened to make this man mad?"

"Well, he was dirty."

"That made you angry with him?"

"I wasn't angry. I just told him he was dirty."

"Were you teasing him, like with me?"

"No."

"Did the man want to hear you tell him he was dirty?"

"It made him mad."

"Like Bethie's mother when you told her to get out of the room?"

He nodded, yes.

"Do you know what I think? I think what you said to these adults was rude."

"Is that bad?"

"Bad because you got into trouble that you couldn't handle and bad for them because they got so mad at you."

He was open and listening easily to what I was saying so I continued. "I'll tell you what. You know how Big Bird is always explaining what words mean?"

He wrinkled his nose. "You mean, Ernie?"

"Okay, Ernie."

"Yeah." He nodded and fingered his suspenders.

"Well, let's you and me talk about the word *rude*. What you said to Bethie's mom was rude. It was rude to tell Bethie's mom to get out of her own house and it was rude to tell someone you don't know and who doesn't know you that he's dirty."

"They were rude too."

"You were rude first. Would you like me to tell you when you are being rude? Like with Jennifer's mom about her haircut and with other parents when you insult them?"

"Can I be rude to you?"

"No, you know I don't let you say hurtful things to me. When we play that way it's because we both want to and it doesn't hurt. We can kid around because it's fun for both of us. It's when the other person doesn't want to hear those things that it's rude. They get angry and want to hurt back."

After this conversation, whenever Mitch was rude, not just plain old obnoxious, I took him aside and told him so. I watched him and whenever he approached the front door to greet arriving children, for instance, in the morning, I was right behind him.

"You wear funny shoes, Mr. Harvey."

"Mitch, you can't say that," I would draw him aside.

"Why not?"

"It's rude."

"Oh." He went back to the front door. "Mr. Harvey?" he said. "You wear *interesting* shoes."

42

Sara and Rudeness

ITCH."

"What is it now, Joanie?" He looked up, startled and guilty. "Can't you see I'm talking to Sara?"

I had just seen him take a shovel from her.

"And what are you saying to her?" I asked, walking over toward him. It was another sunny afternoon, and until that moment, I had been enjoying watching all the squirrels playing in our trees. We were outside standing by the bark box.

"He wants . . ." Sara started to say.

"Be quiet, Sara. I am trying to tell Joanie something."

"Sorry."

Mitch, now with both hands on Sara's shoulders, said, "What I am trying to tell you, Sara, is when you're *finished* with the shovel—"

Sara interrupted, "I want the shovel."

169

"Don't interrupt me when I'm talking to you and take your fingers out of your mouth."

Sara obeyed but she looked perplexed.

Mitch looked at me and back to Sara and said, "What I want you to know is—look at me, Sara—I want the shovel when you're done with it, okay?"

Sara now had both hands to her ears.

"Sara! Listen to me when I'm speaking to you."

She grinned but kept both hands over her ears. Mitch began to shake her by the shoulders, hollering, "Sara! You sure are rude."

Sara looked unhappy.

I said, "Mitch, that's enough. Let go of Sara and find your own shovel."

Mitch let go but started to say something to Sara, who was still covering her ears.

"Enough talking," I said.

But Mitch prevailed. He said to Sara, "You are rude and dumb. I know that."

Then he looked over at me and advised, "You are rude too. Not dumb, but very rude."

Sara suddenly handed the shovel to Mitch. Mitch, now surprised, but still angry, said, "You're still rude, Sara, but not so dumb."

43

Creating a
Generous Heart

BEFORE THERAPY, Danny ate rapidly, staying at it until he overate. He stuffed and chewed and stuffed before swallowing, intent upon getting food off his plate and into his mouth. He'd ask, "When I finish this will there be more?" Afraid that there wouldn't be enough, he was always hurrying to get more. His sense of "not enough" also caused him difficulty in other situations. Even a simple question like "What did you do on Saturday, Dan?" would be answered with, "I'm not going to tell you."

For about three months, Barbara took him aside once a week to bake cookies or cakes. He was allowed to eat as much as he wanted and take home the rest or share with others after naptime.

We wanted Danny to know, as we wanted all our children to know: there is enough in the world.

For weeks he stuffed and hoarded. Then he began to invite selected children to help bake and began to share with them. Then one day he finally decided to share with all the others. Distributing a cookie to each child was like tearing a piece out of himself. He got through it, but it upset him and he took the entire next batch home.

His progress continued, as he was allowed to stuff himself first and share whatever was left over. During this period his approach to meals became less intense. He began to eat only a first helping, more slowly and with more enjoyment. Gradually, he became more generous in other aspects of his day too.

Daycare is neutral territory. Everything belongs to everyone. When the children bring a toy from home, which they often do, they decide if they're going to share it or not. The idea is, when you don't have to share, you are free to choose to lend a toy out and you can also choose to take it back.

Children will even let someone else take a precious toy home, when they are allowed the choice. When forced to share, a child may feel like everything is going away. He or she may become more possessive as a result, rather than more generous.

Sharing is complicated for children, more so than it is for adults. Children have relationships with their toys. As a child, you give so much love to your doll that it becomes more than a doll. You have spent so many miles with your green truck over all this rough territory. You and your truck are more together than just a truck. And then a stranger comes and you suddenly have to share your green truck. Sharing means that you have to let this little person come and take this green truck and do whatever he wants to do with it. And he might get it all wrong. He might break it. Or turn it upside down in a way that it is not supposed to be. What then?

Another reason it is complicated is because children understand things between the ages of two and five by repetition and practice. That's why in Kate's play-drama the children would spend six months doing "The Three Little Pigs" or "Cinderella" over and over again. Likewise, children practice all the time giving away and taking back. What they're dealing with is not just sharing, but also separating. They are also very ambivalent at this age about independence and dependence. And they feel very dependent upon the things that they play with.

We, as parents, expect our children to share their things with others. This is a misconception about how we become generous. This is always an issue for parents. And we say to them what we said to Dan's parents, "We are not insisting that Dan share at this moment; what we're interested in is helping him to develop a *generous nature.*"

We encouraged this in Dan by helping him to develop an attitude about how what belongs to him is used. At our daycare, a child has the right to say, "I don't want you to play with my truck but you can play with something else." The child who doesn't even get the opportunity to say, "I don't want you to play with my truck," can't imagine offering something else instead.

Over the years, the children have developed a phrase, "Mine from my house." If a child is looking at a book and another child comes over and says, "That's mine from my house," he will drop it like a hot potato. It's like magic. They develop a respect for ownership.

At first, Daniel could not understand this concept. He borrowed two trucks, a toy gas station, and a doll from us to take home. When he brought them back and left them on the floor, he cried when he noticed Harry playing with it. "Mine," he said. "Mine from my house."

I said to him, "When you bring your lunch box or your car to school and you don't want others to play with them, that's when you say 'mine from my house.' "

"But I did too bring those from my house this morning."

"But they have to be yours. Not borrowed stuff."

"Oh," he said, still upset, still unclear.

One morning, he brought a bag full of stuff from his

house. Norma apologetically asked if it was all right. We said, "Yes." Danny didn't share any of his assortment of cars, stuffed animals, trucks, etc. We heard, "No, mine from my house," all morning. There were so many of his toys scattered all over the place that the children got confused about whose was whose.

It was time for lunch and I was cleaning up. I asked Danny to gather all his things into his bag to be put on the shelf. As he did it, I said, "Now do you think you understand 'mine from my house'?"

"I think so," he said. And he never had trouble with it again.

We also convince our children that there is plenty. Plenty of people who love them. Plenty of love, so as not to run out, in each of us. Plenty of food in our cupboards and refrigerator. We always have more than we'll use most of the time. For example, Danny had a habit of eating four Yami yogurt pushups one right after another. He told us that if he didn't eat them now, there wouldn't be any more later. But gradually he learned, there's plenty. He began to slow down and sometimes he'd eat two Yami yogurt bars instead of four.

Only when a child is convinced that there is abundance can he or she afford to give a little, or a lot, away. And sharing with another *is* giving it away. A turn, a bite, a greeting— whatever one receives from another is a little bit that the giver no longer has. And he or she must be convinced that there is enough before he can give some away.

This may seem indulgent on our part. But we don't equate a child's wanting with greediness or getting spoiled. What actually happens is that when children want something and they get it, they become less demanding. Greediness is the result of deprivation.

Derek and Joel, aged four, have a favorite Wonder Horse. We have three other Wonder Horses but none of the others holds any value whatsoever for them. Derek rides the favorite while Joel sits and watches. Then Derek relinquishes his turn and watches while Joel rides.

One morning I came upon Derek and Joel beating their favorite horse with shovels.

"Why?" I asked.

"We're going to kill him. He causes too much trouble."

Even with four horses, there isn't enough. We cannot always make things perfect for children. And that's okay. It's enough that we know we try.

44

The Making of
a Friendship

I HATE YOU," DANNY SAID.

He and Mitch were at the kitchen table sharing a dozen or so cookies Danny had made with Barbara during naptime. The other children were in the playroom with Kate. I walked into the kitchen and saw that Danny was close to tears but holding his own with Mitch. Since his work with Dr. Dru, he had begun to change from a shy little boy who couldn't make friends to one who could aggressively reach out and ask for what he needed.

"You are selfish," Mitch said, flushed and mad. "I can have more until they are all gone. You said so."

"I want to keep these. I want to take them home." Since Danny was new at sharing, he became frightened when the cookies were almost all gone. He panicked and grabbed the plate. Mitch was struggling to get it back when Danny saw me walk in the room and slapped Mitch's face. Then he ran away to the front hall—with the cookies.

I walked over to Mitch, pulled out one of the benches, sat down, and took him in my arms and comforted him. When he stopped crying, he said, "I hate him. He always changes his mind. I am never going to share with him ever." He raised his voice. "Do you hear that, Danny. Never!"

Danny didn't answer.

I got up and went to Danny. At first he just sat on the sofa in the other room, leafing through a book, acting like he didn't want to discuss it. Finally, I said, "I know that I don't have to talk to you about slapping Mitch's face because you're not apt to do that again."

He looked up at me with clear eyes and said, "Oh."

"I just wanted you to know that I talked to Mitch about how difficult it was for you to not be able to control the cookies going away and you needed to do something desperate because you couldn't find anything else to do."

"Oh," Danny said again, still looking directly into my eyes. Then we sat side by side for a few moments.

"I'm wondering how you two could make up."

"I want to."

"I think Mitch is still mad."

"I'm not."

"I think Mitch is still mad because he thinks he has been wronged."

Danny sat there for a few moments and thought about it. Then he said, "I could talk to him."

"Good idea." He got up from the sofa and walked toward the kitchen. He was getting to be a tall $3\frac{1}{2}$-year-old, thin and long. I listened.

DANNY: (*to Mitch*) "I could bring more cookies tomorrow and share more."

MITCH: "Oh yeah, well, I don't want to share with you any more. I'll bring more cookies than you and eat them all myself."

Silence.

MITCH: "Do you want to draw? I hate Kate."

DANNY: "Me too. Let's draw."

45

"I Only Have
One Memory"

Y OU CAN'T RIDE BIKES BETTER than I can," Sara taunted
out on the play yard. She was always very feisty
with Mitch when they first started playing.

"I can too. I can ride faster than you," Mitch
would answer.

"No, you can't."

If it wasn't Sara who knew how to do something best,
it was Mitch. "I'm going to swing." Most of their play was
one-upmanship.

"Well, I can swing better than you."

"I made up this game. You have to do it my way."

"I do not. I can make up a better game."

"No, you can't!"

But then Mitch would push and push until he made Sara
cry. "I don't care if it is your game, I hate you and I'm not
going to be your friend."

"Who cares? I don't like you anyway."

Then Sara would get very red in the face and shake her short curly black hair like a little poodle and say, "You make me unhappy. You make me cry," she'd say, jumping up and down. "You make me so unhappy."

"Well," he'd say, "you make me unhappy too."

"No, you make me much more unhappy than I ever make you."

"Well, it's your fault."

"No, it's not, see—you're making me unhappy."

Then he'd stare at her. "Well, okay, if you let me say it's my game then I'll let you be the queen."

She'd think about it for a moment and then finally answer, "Okay."

"Are you happy?" he'd then ask, for underneath it all Mitch really did have a good heart.

So they'd play. But at some point he'd invariably say, "Your queen is a dum-dum. I'm going to be king." Sara would of course cry and Mitch would be worried, but not enough so to let her be the hero.

For Mitch, their relationship was beginning to feel like "we're-stuck-together-and-there's-nothing-in-the-world-we-can-do-about-it." And his actions were "But I just want you to know I don't like being around you. Actually, I really hate it."

But for Sara, it was a very different situation. She loved Mitch. And she wanted to do everything with him.

Mitch and Danny played together once a week when they sat out from Kate's play-drama. But because of Mitch's exclusiveness with Sara, he seldom interacted with Danny at other times. However, as time went on, they would exchange information or plan what they would do together the next Thursday. And as they spent time together they gradually sought each other out at other times. If Sara was absent for a day they spent the whole time together.

The old pattern of Mitch's getting his own way in play

didn't work with Danny. The threats of "I won't be your best friend" were virtually ignored by Danny who sometimes still only half wanted to play anyway. Mitch now had to draw upon his own good resources to seduce Danny into an activity. This was very hard for Mitch for he was used to an entirely different system with Sara, but on the other hand, he really wanted to play with Danny.

"Danny!" I heard Mitch yell one day. "Don't go away. Come back. I will not give you a fat lip. I promise."

"Danny?" he said again. "Here, you can have the truck. You are not such a dum-dum after all."

Mitch was learning to become somewhat gracious because it was the only way Dan would accept him.

Almost daily, then, Mitch began to have to make a decision—Dan or Sara?

"Why not both?" I asked one day.

"I can't play with two people at the same time, dummy."

When Mitch chose Sara, Danny just shrugged his shoulders and did other things. Once the decision was made, Mitch was never tempted to change his mind. But when Mitch chose Danny, Sara was devastated. She would cry on and off during the day and find it difficult to involve herself very deeply in play with others. In fact, reading became the only substitute that she really found satisfying.

When he chose Danny, Mitch could see how unhappy and lonely Sara was for him. He'd call her crybaby and make fun of her. And the next day, when he chose her, he would tell her how much he hated her crying. "If you don't stop it, I will always hate you and never be your friend ever again."

I sat down with Mitch on the bench and talked to him about how he was treating Sara when she was already so unhappy. "I don't want her to cry," he said. "I hate it and it makes me hate her even more."

I looked at him, so sturdy in his favorite striped T-shirt and jeans with green suspenders. "Then why can't you play with both your friends?" I asked.

He looked at me incredulously. "I only have one memory, that's why."

46

The Spaceship Ride

YEA, YEA, MITCH, COME AND GET ME." Sara had her tongue out, fingers in her ears. Mitch didn't rise to the challenge, just waved his arms and walked on. "Mitch," Sara screamed, running toward him. "Yea, yea, can't catch me, dummy!"

"Sara, come here," I called.

She was surprised and looked sheepish. She stood there.

"Sara," I said again, "come here."

She came toward me. She said, "I am tired . . . are you?"

"Am I what?"

Sara said, "I am tired, aren't you?"

I said, "No, I am not tired. Sit here by me."

She sat down. She sighed. "I am too tired to talk."

I said, "Are you too tired to listen?"

She said, "Yes," in a very tired voice as she sat beside me wearing her favorite very purple jumpsuit.

I said, "Well, then, we'll just sit here quietly for a while."

As time went by, playing with Danny had become much more satisfying to Mitch than playing with Sara. Instead of the "Shut up! I'm better than you, dum-dum" "No, you aren't" sort of interchange that he had with Sara, it became "Do you want to see my anthill?" "Sure." It was a much more challenging and growing relationship.

For Sara, on the other hand, all of Mitch's most fearful threats were coming true. "I'll never play with you again. I hate you. You're not my best friend."

After a little while, Mitch came over. "Joanie," he said, fingering one of his suspenders. "I don't have anything to do." He had been wandering about for a while.

"Sit here by me and see if we can think of something you'd like to do."

He sat down beside me. Sara was still sitting on the other side.

"Let's travel off into space," I said.

Mitch thought for a moment and then said, pointing at Sara, "Is she coming?"

I said, "Let's pretend this bench is a moon ship and we are traveling to the moon."

"Have we left yet?" Sara said.

"It's up to you."

She jumped up. "Let's say we haven't left yet and I'll go get M&Ms at the store to take with us 'case we get hungry." She ran off.

Mitch said, "I bet she gets pine cones."

"We'll see. Is there something you want to get for the trip?"

"I wish she wasn't going with us," he said, looking at me. "Where's Danny?"

"He's sick today."

"I wish Danny were here."

Sara came back with small pieces of bark, excited to have found M&Ms.

I said, "What else should we take with us?"

Mitch said, "I would take stuff if I don't have to share it with you." He looked over at Sara.

"If you get stuff to eat you have to share," Sara said.

"I'm not getting stuff," he said.

"I'll be right back," Sara said. "I am going to get drinks." She ran off.

Mitch looked at me and said, "Let's blast off now."

"Without Sara?"

"Yes, before she gets back. I bet she's looking for pine cones."

Sara returned with two pine cones. One for me and one for herself for drinks.

I said, "I am going to the store now."

Both children asked me, "What for?"

"M&Ms and one drink and a surprise."

They waited for me, watching what I was doing. I got some small pieces of bark and one pine cone and three rocks. I gave Mitch one pine cone and a handful of M&Ms. I gave each of us a rock which I said was an ice cream bar. We sat and licked our rocks.

"I'm hungry," Mitch said.

"Me too," Sara agreed.

"That's good," I said. "Lunch is ready, see?" As they looked up, Barbara called us for lunch.

This is a very complicated technique of mine called getting through the next fifteen minutes. I live in the moment too with them. Sometimes I can do no more than sit there as they go through it with each other. For Mitch and Sara, it was clearly a difficult time. We all know when something is over, it's over. But, unfortunately, it's usually not over with for two people at the same time. Still, there was nothing wrong with Mitch outgrowing Sara. He didn't do this on purpose to hurt her. He just wanted to get in his spaceship and go. He wanted to be free.

47

Sister Lizard

KATE SAT DOWN ON THE FLOOR, tossed her hair, and said, "Well, what's the story for today, morning glories?"

The children who were best at all this would name the stories. " 'Cinderella'!" they would say. "No, 'The Three Little Pigs'!" "No!" someone else would say, " 'The Three Bears'!" "No, a scary one! A scary one!"

Maggie, who was very shy and timid, a pale little girl with very fine straight blond hair, would always slink away when Kate came, hiding under the table next to the couch.

But this one day, Kate sort of slunk right over to where she was underneath the table and said, "Are you a little salamander?" She was kneeling under the table, staring at the little pale blond in pink overalls.

Maggie said, "No, I'm a lizard."

"Can I play lizards with you?"

"Well, yes."

185

"Can I come to your house?"

"Well, yes."

Kate got under the table with her. "What are you doing?"

"Well, we're eating."

"What are we eating?"

"Lizard food, silly."

"Oh, well. I'm hungry and I want some too."

So Maggie began to feed Kate, the lizard. Soon enough all the children wanted to join in.

"I want to be a lizard, too," Mitch said. He had mellowed toward Kate as he matured and was once again participating in play-drama.

Maggie didn't say a thing but hid deeper under the table. Though Mitch was making yet another attempt at being the good guy he still turned out to be, in action, very arrogant. Consequently, in this play, he became the most boorish lizard around. "I'll get the lizard food for you. You're too stupid to find it yourself."

Once the lizard game got started, the children played it for weeks on end. They each set up their own households and had their own picnics and celebrations. Kate always wanted food so Maggie fed her often. And as Maggie got braver, Kate would say, "Why do we have to stay here in this hole underneath this table?"

"Because we're safe here," Maggie answered. "You don't have to go out there because we have everything we need right here."

"But I want a banana," Kate said.

"Here's a banana," Maggie answered.

"But I want some rain to fall on me."

"There's a hole in the roof."

No matter what it was, Maggie had it all together underneath the table.

As I sat on the couch and observed, I thought staying underneath that table is exactly what they should have done until Maggie gained enough confidence herself to go out there in the middle of the fray where the other children were.

However, Kate began to think, "I can get her out of here." But she didn't say a word to me.

One day, as Mitch struggled with his desire to be a good lizard and his greater need to stay a bad one, and Meredith refused to give up her spot in one of the lizard caves, Maggie was under the table in her hole, as usual. She felt totally safe from Mitch and the others as she hid there with her sister lizard, Kate. Maggie knew the rules. Maggie herself was in charge of the game. Consequently, because she trusted Kate, she continued to open up to her. Then Kate said, "I want us to go out into the world."

Maggie smiled, saying, "Well, what do you want?"

"I want something that we don't have here."

Maggie cocked her head, saying, "Well, what is it?"

"Well, I can only show it to you," Kate said.

I was sitting on the sofa as usual when I began to feel a little troubled about where Kate was leading Maggie. It was so unlike her to intervene in a child's play. As a matter of fact, I had discussed with her at length my second thoughts about the intervening I had done with Jeffie about Greeney. Kate and I had both agreed that redirecting a child's play was the therapist's job, not ours.

"Please, little sister," she said. "Come with me out into the world . . . I want to show you something, and you won't be afraid."

"Well," Maggie said, "what is it?"

"I can show you." Then Kate began to use all her skill as an adult to get Maggie to come out in the world. She finally said when she got her out from under the table, "See, it's just this little pot, and we're just going to catch some fish for dinner, which we don't have now."

"Oh, that," Maggie said. "We have a pot at home. We have a fish like that. Come on, I'll show you," and she started to go back into the hole.

"No. No," Kate said. "We'll stay here. I want us to stay out here."

Maggie looked carefully around the playroom and then directly at Kate. "I don't want to play," she said.

And she never played with Kate again.

48

Jason

SHE WAS ALIVE but still in a coma," he said to me excitedly. "*And* she was pregnant. The question was, could a baby be born to a mother in a coma?"

Charleton and I were sitting next to each other at the dinner table surrounded by candlelight. He's a friend who is an obstetrician at Hamilton Hospital. At a dinner party that Carol Washburn gave, he was telling us about a patient of his, four months pregnant, who recently had an aneurysm, a stroke. He went to her husband about terminating the pregnancy. The husband said, "I'm not going to do it. I think there's a chance she is going to be okay, and in any event, I want this child." So Charleton said, "Okay, if that's what you want to do, I'm with you. We'll do it together."

As he talked, I could smell roast lamb and mint and feel the polished linen under my fingertips. There were other people at the party but all I remember is Charleton's tan, lined face and very animated black eyes as he told me this story.

Whenever a nurse went into the room to feed his patient or change the IV, he or she would talk aloud about what they were doing. Charleton wanted as much information given her as possible, even though she couldn't participate.

He came in each day and talked to her. He told her what nutrition they were giving her, how the baby was doing, and as much other medical information as he had about her situation. A physical therapist came in to keep her muscles toned. And each evening, her husband, Scott, came in to talk to her for an hour or so as he ate his dinner near her.

No one knew, at that time, how much brain damage there was, or what she was able to take in, but they all created as normal an atmosphere as possible. What no one realized at the time was also how much they were actually nurturing this child. Whatever the mother was able to assimilate became the emotional climate for this baby.

In fact, later on, Dr. Dru had to glean what it actually was like for Jason in utero while his mother was unconscious for so long. We know much about the developing infant—that it dreams, hears, and responds—but what about its emotional climate? This is the question Dru had to answer to help Jason—what happened to this growing child hidden in his mother's too real darkness?

Charleton couldn't stop talking about all this at the party. He was thrilled that such a thing was possible. I rushed right home and told Barbara immediately.

She was in the kitchen getting a Pepsi out of the refrigerator and turned around when she said, "We're going to get this kid."

I said, "No, we aren't."

She said, "Yeah, we are, we're going to have this kid, it's in the stars." And she laughed.

49

Halloween

I LOVE HALLOWEEN, not as much as Christmas, of course, but I enjoy the time of leaves—how shimmery the fall is in Oakland on our street with the crackling colorful birch leaves everywhere. I have saved wonderful decorations over the years and I bring everything I own out. Skeletons hang on the front door, witches from the playroom ceiling, paper pumpkins everywhere. One year I didn't have to put up my favorite cobweb and black widow spider because right outside our playroom window a large spider had spun an amazing silver web.

Ana at $3\frac{1}{2}$. What a wonder this little girl had become! She was still often on medication but rarely absent. Even when she was feverish she begged to come to daycare. She became very impatient whenever her mother approached her, putting

191

a hand on her forehead or watching her too carefully, looking for signs of illness.

"I am *not* sick. I am going to Joanie and Barbara's to-day." It seemed as if she wanted to come so badly that she willed her body to behave.

Because Halloween was just around the corner when Ana's parents came over for a visit with Barbara and me, they brought with them the materials for the last touch to her witch costume—a tall cone-shaped black hat which still needed to be cut out. Her mother measured and sewed as Ana danced about, practicing her witchy attitude. Then she put on the hat and took it off as she directed where the sparkles would be.

All the children were talking about what they would be on Halloween. Most of them were very decisive. Tina, Jennifer, and Meredith were going to be beautiful princesses, no surprise there. Terry wanted to be a doctor and Joey a clown and Joel chose to be a cowboy. We had one ghost, two pirates, even a Peter Pan. Mitch was trying to decide whether to come as a monster or a pirate, which made things very complicated for Sara for she had decided to "go" as Mitch. Mitch's friend Danny chose to be a baseball player.

Ana and Sally were going to be witches. Sally had a huge spider web on her hat and a terrible, funny black spider dangling from its peak. Ana didn't want to have that; she said, however, that sparkles were meant to be *very* scary. But she knew they were really beautiful. Her reason for being a witch in the first place, rather than a beautiful princess like her other friends, was to be scary enough to frighten all the other spooks out there. After all, if she weren't scary herself she might be someone who was scared and that wouldn't do.

As for Barbara and me, we were a bit anxious about the weather and about the events we couldn't control—Ana's health being one among them. The year before she had been too sick to join us. As the day got closer, she continued to do whatever was best for her per her parents and our instructions—took yucky medicine, napped with a vaporizer, got enough rest, ate good food, took vitamins, and wore what we told her to wear. Ever cooperative, she trusted that we knew best. Come what may, this year she was going out on Halloween because she remembered how left out she felt the year before. She was a bit anxious about her costume, though. It was modified daily—too short, too long, too full, too skimpy. The hat, however, she left alone.

Halloween was Friday and on the Monday before we were hanging more ghosts from the ceiling, witches on the walls, and discussing our jack-o-'lantern. Should it be scary or friendly? In-between felt too bland, therefore boring. During the week we cut construction paper pumpkins or drew orange ones with all kinds of faces. By Wednesday half the children still wanted a fierce pumpkin, the other half a happy one. By Thursday, we were knee deep in practice pumpkins and no closer to agreement.

What to do? Someone had given us a huge pumpkin from the nearby pumpkin festival. It must have weighed seventy-five pounds. It would be easy to have two pumpkins, I suggested, one bad and one good. But where would we find a mate to the one we had? I had never seen such a large one anywhere. So we didn't cut the big one on the front porch at all. We found two others of equal size and we cut one frightening face—huge painted eyebrows, pupils askew, and a great round mouth with many teeth—and a friendly one— happy smile, lines on either side of the mouth, crinkly eyes, funny nose. We placed them on each side of the great one and were satisfied.

Ana continued to talk about being a witch and she and Sally practiced scaring people. They knew exactly where they were going. I had constructed a series of houses of construction paper with little doors that actually opened so that the children could practice knocking on the doors. When each door was opened there might be a skeleton behind it or a ghost so they knew exactly what they were in for. And they all loved it. So every day Ana practiced.

The plan was that we wouldn't do anything during the day about Halloween. But at the end of the day the kids would all stay and we would have dinner. Every Halloween we had hot dogs, potato chips, Hawaiian punch, and some candy—all the junk we ordinarily shun. Then we'd all go out of the house together in a great long Halloween parade and visit a number of the friendly houses on our dead-end street. The children and I usually loved it, except for this particular Halloween. . . .

50

"She Insists Upon a Clown Face, Even Though She Has Fairy Wings"

ITCH STILL COULDN'T DECIDE between being a monster or a pirate. So the morning of Halloween, he brought both costumes to our house. Earlier, when he couldn't decide on which costume to wear, Sara's mother simply asked Mitch's mom for some of his clothes. So his striped T-shirt, jeans, and a pair of red suspenders became Sara's costume. Obviously, this was a very powerful situation for her. Mitch, on the other hand, didn't care if she wore his clothes or not. He was entirely involved with his new best friend, Danny, and on deciding what to wear.

Halloween morning we were calm. I remember, because the children told me so many times. Our agenda was to stay as calm as we could all morning, have a spooky lunch, a sound nap, and a good play outside. Then instead of going

195

home at 5:30, everyone would stay for the party. All went according to plan until the afternoon when it was time to paint faces and put on costumes. Barbara and I had helpers, bless them, two parents and Karen and Laura, my grown daughters. We were well organized but given the task, it was pretty hectic. Department and food store bags were thrown everywhere, each with a child's name on it. Many had instructions stapled to the bags. "Please put tights on before costume and over shoes." Or "Enclosed please find five colors of makeup; she insists upon a clown face even though she has fairy wings. Try to talk her out of it."

Danny had on his baseball outfit with its red cap, baseball bat, and leather mitt and Mitch had finally decided to be a pirate in spite of his continuing attempts to play the hero.

Kate came that afternoon to paint faces. She set up a large mirror in the playroom so that each child could see to direct her.

Mitch's turn came and Kate said, "Okay, Mitch, teeth and scars and thick black eyebrows?"

He looked at his reflection in the mirror. "I want to be a prince," he said.

"What?" she said, looking up from her bottles of paint.

"I want to be a prince."

Recovering, Kate said, as she wiped the tears from her eyes and got out the right paint, "Well, I'll have cold cream ready in case you change your mind."

"Kate, you sure are dumb," Mitch said. "Why are you crying?"

As each child finished being dressed and made up they went into the kitchen for hot dogs. Finally, when there were more children in the kitchen than the playroom, I noticed I hadn't seen Ana. I looked up to see a Macy's bag still hanging on a hook in the hall and a very tall and sparkly witch's hat hung from elastic on the same hook. But where was Ana?

As I walked through the hall and went toward the

kitchen, I noticed a lump hidden under the two pillows on the couch.

"Are you ready to get into your costume, Ana?" I asked the lump.

"No, Joanie," came a muffled voice.

"How about some supper?"

Out popped Ana's head from under the pillow. She jumped up and followed me into the kitchen. Ana still loved meals best of all. Two hot dogs, lots of catsup, many chips, and two glasses of Hawaiian punch later, the rest of the children were lining up at the door as Kate passed out trick-or-treat bags. Ana was still eating, planted there at the table.

"Well, Ana," Barbara smiled. She noticed her without costume but said nothing. "Are you ready for trick or treat?"

"Yeah, I'm ready," and she got her trick-or-treat bag from Kate and ran over to Sally and said, "I'm a witch."

Sally, in her elaborate little witch's costume with a spider hanging down from a great witch hat, said, "Me too."

There Ana stood with her playclothes full of catsup and hot dogs and punch. Sally held out her hand to her and she took it and they marched out into the night. It was Ana's Halloween.

51

Our Last Public Halloween

THE PRINCESSES WERE FIRST out the door. They were the eldest and knew the ropes and were first at most things. We were all out the door now and gathered on the porch. It was dark, the pumpkins lit with candles and sinister-appearing. Even the friendly one looked eerie. We looked across the street to the house which was our first stop. There was a skeleton on the door and a ghost swinging back and forth from the porch ceiling. There were two ferocious jack-o'-lanterns on each side of the stairs, and there in the window, the only source of regular light in the house, was a witch's face, her eyes and nostrils aglow.

The six adults turned on their flashlights. We were ready to go. Some children were and some weren't. The older ones held each other's hands. The younger ones wanted to be carried. We began to lumber down the street, like one long multicolored Halloween snake. The princesses followed Barbara, who was in the lead, carrying Joel. Her flashlight shone on the porch stairs. I was next, carrying Crissy. Following me came a baseball player and a pirate, and after them came a little girl in red suspenders, a striped shirt, her face painted like a prince. I turned and shined the light back up the stairs. The rest of the children just stood there.

"Come on!" I said crossly.

They just stood there.

"What is it?"

"We can't see." Of course, their masks! I pushed the front children's masks up to cover the top of their heads and called on the other adults to do the same for those children wearing masks. Finally we were assembled at the sidewalk, our next stop before going across the street. Everyone was quiet as we stood still, and Jennifer, one of the princesses, asked, "Whose houses are we going to again?"

"Are you getting worried?" I asked.

"It's spooky out here. It's dark and it's different."

"Don't worry, Jen," I said. "We know who lives across the street. Remember Penny and Robert and their baby? Let's go. There's nothing to be afraid of."

Alert! We're going to cross. We trudged across the street toward the neighbor's front door, Barbara and I and the other four adults trying to corral the littlest ones as they looked into their bags and the masks fell back down onto their faces. We sort of pushed the children past the jack-o'-lanterns and under the hanging ghost, who on closer inspection, was hanging by a rope from its neck and dripping blood from various wounds. We could no longer—thank God—see the witch in the window.

No one knocked on the door. Most of the children were looking back toward our house, that is, those whose eyes were not riveted on the ghost.

"Children," I said. "Remember what we practiced. Just knock on the door."

Tina, aged four, another princess, asked, looking back toward our house, "Have my parents come to your house yet?"

So I took the initiative and knocked. "Say trick or treat," I said. The door opened. The children were mute. All stepped backward hurriedly and managed to unbalance a parent who had to step backward as well and almost fell back down the porch stairs.

Out from behind the door came Penny with a great smile and a basket full of candy bars and bubble gum. Everyone danced forward at once, the little ones struggling to get out of our arms and into the candy basket. I breathed for the first time in several minutes and began directing, "Say thank you, say Happy Halloween," and all the children did. The door closed and we eagerly went up the street two houses to our next stop.

More fierce pumpkins. An electrified skeleton which now no one noticed as they pushed to the door, everyone wanting to knock.

"Trick or treat!" shouted everyone.

More knocking, more yelling, "Trick or treat!"

An elderly couple, who loved us all, opened the door and held out packages of popcorn balls and homemade cookies carefully prepared for just this moment.

"Let us look at these goblins," they pleaded. "Oh my goodness, a ghost. Oh no, a pirate. Is that Santa Claus? Well now, is that the cutest thing! What beautiful princesses," and on and on. Each child noticed, each appreciated. I was feeling more confident by the moment. The children were straining to get on with it.

"Let's get more candy, let's do a trick! Let's scare everybody, come on, come on!"

We went on toward our next scheduled stop, the house at the end of the street. But as we rushed by, someone said, "Look, there's a house, Joanie." Someone else said, "They're home. They have pumpkins." "They have candy." I turned around to Barbara and called, "How about here?"

"I guess so," she answered as the children bounded up the stairs to the decorated door. Barbara didn't like deviations from our plans but was willing occasionally to change gears.

Bang. Bang. Bang. The older children were knocking before we were up the steps with the little ones. The door flung open. A seven-foot-tall skeleton with a fully articulated jaw, opening and closing, opening and closing, came toward us. The children backed away. He still came forward. Everyone cried, dove for us, running straight up our legs. We had kids on our heads, up on legs, on our backs. There didn't seem to be a foot on the ground. We were forced backward by them. As we moved back, the seven-foot skeleton continued onto the porch and toward us. We were moving away from this man in one colorfully screaming glob of kids, parents, spilling bags, and he was still coming toward us!

We finally all fled down the stairs. As we fled, we could see huge witches, ghosts, ghouls, and vampires behind him.

The three older kids made a beeline for our house. They were up the stairs and into the house before I got there. "Lock the door! Lock the door!" they screamed. I was running right after them. "Lock the door, Joanie!"

I tried to tell them, "It was a Halloween party." But they weren't going to buy that, they knew what they saw—the thing was real, it was going to eat them, and they barely got away from it. I locked the door. As far as they were concerned, they were not going out again and they were not going to open the door. Soon enough, the rest of the children, the younger ones, came back with the other parents and banged on our door.

I opened it and went out onto the porch. For the younger children who live only in the moment, that experience was already in the past and they were in the present, standing on the porch, wanting to go back out. These older children behind the door who knew they had a past and a future were not going out. "Leave us here! Leave us here!" they yelled through a crack in the door. The older children had enough sense to know the seven-foot skeleton was still there; the little ones thought he was gone because they couldn't see him anymore. I went out with the younger group and asked my daughter Karen to stay in the house with them.

When we finished up Halloween we came back to the house. Karen said that she had had the worst time with other neighborhood trick-or-treaters because the four-year-old girls, who had hidden in our house, wouldn't let her open the door.

She had to holler through the door to the other trick-or-treaters, "Come back, we're not ready yet! Come back soon!"

The trick-or-treaters yelled back, "Why don't you just open the door and throw out the candy?"

"We're not ready yet, you come back in a while."

The neighborhood trick-or-treaters took out their frustrations on our pumpkins, smashing the happy one with the fierce one. The huge one was unharmed and stayed with us through Thanksgiving.

I unlocked the front door for the third time for parents because the princesses kept locking it. Tina's father, Dr. Washburn, came in. She threw herself in his arms. As it turned out, he was a godsend because just then Barbara rushed in. Peter Pan was choking on hard candy. She put him in Washburn's surprised arms, saying, "Help! Do something."

Dr. Washburn gently held Joey over his knee as he struggled with the sourball. He tipped him and tipped him and by the third time finally it popped out. He knew how to let gravity work.

Then Barbara went through everybody's bags. The children started screaming at the top of their lungs but she threw away every piece of hard candy and she has continued to do so every Halloween since.

After all of this we decided that next year we would stay at home in costume and eat candy after naptime, which is what we have done ever since. Three of our four neighbors, our Halloween regulars, still bring treats to our house on Halloween afternoon. We only allow soft candy, though. They don't mind; they miss us.

There were some parents who were disappointed because they thought this Halloween was an amazing thing we did. And they were right—too amazing.

52

Seeking Mary's Penis

WE NEED A FLASHLIGHT, can we have a flashlight?" Meredith said excitedly as she came out of the bathroom, and went through the laundry room and into the kitchen where I was making lunch. She was wearing a bright green blouse with nothing else on. "Do you have a flashlight?" she asked.

"Yes," I said. "In the bottom drawer. What are you looking for that you need a light?"

"We're looking for Mary's penis."

"Does Mary have a penis?"

"I don't think so, but her mother told her she has one and we want to find it. She thinks it's inside herself."

Meredith found the flashlight and took it into the bathroom. Ana, Mary, Bramble, and Meredith had been in there for about twenty minutes. There are two potty chairs in there and one adult-sized flush toilet. They prefer the flush toilet when they need to use one. Since they insist upon company whenever they need to go, they usually go as a group.

Earlier, Meredith needed to have a bowel movement, so Ana, Mary, and Bramble accompanied her. Sally, who was not toilet trained yet, wanted to wait for them outside and swing. Meredith used the flush toilet. When Ana got the urge to have a BM, Meredith hurried so that she could use the big toilet.

I can clearly hear what goes on in the bathroom from the kitchen. Meredith hurried and even got off the toilet before she wiped herself as Ana desperately needed to move her bowels. Ana hopped on and Meredith wiped herself. Then Ana moved over a bit so Meredith could put the used toilet paper into the toilet. Now Mary needed to urinate. "Ana, hurry hurry hurry. I have to pee."

Ana: "Pee in the little potty." This was fair as the girls would pee in the potties if the toilet was taken. But since they all "needed" the big toilet for BMs, they would do what they could in the way of hurrying if another had to do a BM. I heard Mary say, "Please, Ana, I hate the little potties."

Nothing.

I heard Mary say urgently, "Ana, I said I have to pee, get off."

Nothing.

"Get off, Ana, I have to do a BM too," Mary says again.

ANA: "You said you had to pee. You didn't say you had to do a BM."

MARY: "I have to do a BM and pee. I forgot."

Nothing.

MARY: "Ana, I'm going to tell Joanie if you don't get off."

Nothing.

Mary, calling to me as she comes into the kitchen,

"Joanie, Joanie, Ana won't let me have a BM. My mother said not to hold BMs and I am getting a stomachache."

I said, "I think Ana will get finished soon with her BM, then you can do yours."

Mary says, as she runs back into the toilet room, "Joanie said you have to get off. It's not good to hold BMs, so get off."

The sound of toilet paper coming off the roll and Mary coming into the kitchen. "Joanie, Ana is wiping herself *ON* the toilet." She is outraged.

I call, "Ana, will you be finished soon?"

Nothing.

"Mary, go see if she's finished."

Mary runs back. Ana off. Mary on. From the toilet, I hear Mary say, "I don't think you are very nice, Ana. You made me wait too long."

ANA: "Well, I don't think you are very nice either, Mary, because I don't think you have to have a BM."
MARY: "I do too have to. You'll see."
ANA: "Well, then, do it."
MARY: "I will."
ANA: "Do it."
MARY: *"I will."*
ANA: "See, you can't."
MARY: "I can too."
ANA: "Then do it."
MARY: "I am."

Silence. Then Ana says, "See, you don't have a BM."

MARY: "I do too."
ANA: (*to Meredith and Bramble*) "Let's go outside."
MARY: "You have to wait for me. I waited for you."
ANA: "No, we don't have to if you take too long."
BRAMBLE: "I am going outside."

MEREDITH: "Me too. I am finished."
  MARY: "Don't go till I do my BM."
    ANA: "You don't have to do a BM, you lied."
  MARY: "I did not."
    ANA: "Let's go."

Mary says to them as she sees them leave and wants them to stay, "Do you want to see my penis?"

MEREDITH: "You don't have a penis. Boys have
          penises, girls have vaginas."
    MARY: "I do too have a penis, my mother said."
     ANA: "Where is it? Let me see it."
    MARY: "I don't know where it is. Look, can you
          find it? It is small, my mother said."

I hear the girls looking.

BRAMBLE: "I don't see a penis. Maybe it's in there."
   MARY: "Maybe."
BRAMBLE: "I can't see up there."
   MARY: "Get a light."

So that's how Meredith got the light from me and Ana turned it on. They tried to find Mary's penis, then Meredith's, and finally Ana's and Bramble's. They were enjoying the search and weren't too disappointed at not finding anything. I went out into the yard and when I returned I met Meredith carrying a pair of pliers into the bathroom. She must have seen them when she opened the drawer for the flashlight. I said, "Meredith, what are you going to do with the pliers?"

Meredith: "Bramble needs to fix something."

This is something else, I thought to myself. I said, "I'll watch."

We went into the bathroom. Meredith gave the pliers to Bramble.

Bramble said, "Thanks," and proceeded to try to fix the buckle on her sandal. I laughed at myself as I walked away.

Lunch was ready so I called the other children in. Finally, I called Mary out of the bathroom. She didn't want to come and kept stalling. Finally everyone was seated, including Mary, and we had lunch. Ana ran in to check for BM in the toilet.

I read to them all until Barbara was ready to take the children to nap. The five little girls were with me, having outgrown their need for a nap, and they decided to draw at the kitchen table. I was at my desk when Mary came to me. She rested her arm on mine and stood beside me. I was writing. I patted her arm, looked up, and smiled at her.

Nothing.

I continued writing. As Mary stood next to me, she was feeling that she wanted to fix things with her friends, but she didn't know how. Her usual way was to promise to do something special later for the one whom she tricked, such as, "I'll bring candy, just for you, tomorrow." Sometimes it was, "I'll be your best friend, come on, just you and me will play." Though the intention was generous, the effect was intrusive to the group, as these girls had begun to like being involved all together. I looked at her. This time she looked up.

"My mama told me little girls have penises like boys only they are smaller."

I asked, "When did you have this conversation?"

She said, "Yesterday when I was looking at Daddy's penis. We talked about how boys have small penises and men's are the same as boys but bigger and I asked her why we had vaginas and she said we had vaginas for penises to fit into when we were women to have babies and that we had little penises too to make it feel good. They think I am lying like about the BM."

I said, "But you're not lying, you just don't really understand what your mom meant about your penis?"

Mary, nodding, said, "Right. I can't find it but she said I had one."

I said, "I think you'll feel better about this when you understand better what she meant."

Mary, taking her arm away from mine, said, "I'll ask her tonight." She left, went back into the kitchen, and said, "Joanie said my mom was right. I just don't understand what she said. I'll ask her tonight and show you where it is to-morrow . . . when I bring candy for just us to share."

The girls said, "Okay, Mary's bringing candy just for us tomorrow. Good."

Pretty clever, I'd say, two birds with one stone.

Frankly, the specific questions about sex that most parents ask me are ones for which I don't have specific answers. "How much time in sex play is normal?" "What kind of sex play is natural?" "What can we morally approve of?" "Should we distract them?" "Are they bored, do we need to provide other activities?" "I feel uncomfortable when she has a friend over and she closes her bedroom door, what should I do?"

My experience with sex play with children is that when it is not normal or natural it is unmistakably clear. The little girls I have known spend time in the bathroom examining themselves and each other. They take their underpants off and watch themselves pee and look at themselves when they are not peeing. They are fascinated with their likenesses and in comparing and examining each other's equipment. A lot of touching is required as they explore this part of their bodies. And they feel pleasure in another's touch. The urge to urinate and move one's bowels physically is also stimulating to a child to further stimulate oneself and others' genitals.

Playing doctor is another stimulation for sexual play. I can remember well the glorious feeling of "having things" done to me by my neighborhood friends. The not knowing what they may do next and the excitement and fantasy about what things they might do was an irresistible pleasure that I did not in any way try to resist. For me there was no wrong or right about it, just the necessity to find a private place where we would not be disturbed or seen and could do it as long as we wanted to.

This privacy that the children seek out at our daycare is the bathroom, the small hall beside the stairs, and the space out of doors between our garage and the neighbor's fence. They feel as I did as a child that they are alone and unseen.

The little boys that I have known seek privacy too to play with their penises. Their play is less explorative and more demonstrative. Aside from noticing and feeling the differences between circumcised and uncircumcised and moving the foreskin up and down, most of the sex play becomes who can pee highest against the garage wall or most accurately into a bucket from the longest distance from it. They may try to pee into another's anus but they are actually trying to pee toward the opening rather than trying to penetrate it.

The touching of one's self for pleasure, directing another's touch to give pleasure, is the usual narcissistic approach children have to sex play. "Do me, then I'll do you." "You be the doctor and do stuff to me." This openness to feeling pleasure and demanding it from others allows one to learn by experience what is pleasurable and what isn't. Meanwhile, attitudes about one's body are developing as a result of the experience. If we as adults believe that this knowledge is important, then we will have an attitude of acceptance that will be transmitted to our children. It communicates, "My body is okay." If, on the other hand, we are fearful or anxious about what is happening, the attitude transmitted is, "This part of me is somehow not okay. Therefore, I don't feel okay about my whole self in the world."

We don't have to be watchful and attentive when they are behind closed bedroom or bathroom doors. If we know they are in there and that the door is shut is awareness enough.

In all my years I have had only one experience of sex play that I couldn't let go to its natural finish. One little boy, years ago, wanted to play at sex beyond any of his friends' interest in continuing. He was at first only trying to get someone between the garage wall and the neighbor's fence. As time went by he wanted kids to put sticks in his rectum. He would come to us and insist that someone play doctor in this way with him. No one would, he said, and we actively disapproved of what he was requesting. We talked with his parents, with him present. And we helped him direct his sexual energy where we could let it go.

Since this experience has been the only negative one in fifteen years, I feel relaxed about this aspect of children's play. It is unusual that one needs to stop or frustrate or redirect the expression of sexual feelings in children. It is my experience that it is very clear when the play is harmful.

The next morning when Mary came in, she went directly to Ana and Meredith and Bramble and said, "I have candy and I have a 'litteris. It's like a little penis but it doesn't look like one, that's why we couldn't find it. Also, it's right on top, so we don't need a flashlight. When Sally comes I'll show you all my 'litteris and we'll find yours. Cause it's not just me that has it. Mama said all girls have them."

    ANA: " 'Litteris?"
    MARY: "Right, 'litteris."
    ANA: (*pleased*) "Really?"
    MARY: "Really, and we'll eat the jelly beans I brought
           too."

53

Look at Crissy. Ha Ha

OOK AT CRISSY. Ha ha," Mitch said to Crissy. She had spaghetti everywhere—in her hair, on the table, running down her T-shirt. She was using the fork in one of her hands and all the fingers of the other to try to shovel it in her mouth. But the next time spaghetti was served, Crissy ate it without sauce and only a little cheese. Mitch's remark had struck a nerve and she didn't want to call attention to herself.

I drew Mitch aside and said, "You noticed last week that Crissy gets full of spaghetti sauce when she eats. What I want you also to notice is that now Crissy is not enjoying eating her spaghetti as she was before. *I* noticed that you eat spaghetti with a minimum of mess. You're older and have more experience eating it. I want Crissy to have as much practice as you've had."

This was my way of letting Mitch know that his teasing had made Crissy self-conscious about eating and that I didn't like it. But it also let him know that I was aware of his progress since he brought attention to it.

The next time Crissy asked for spaghetti without sauce, Mitch noticed and said to her, "I used to make a *BIG* mess with spaghetti but I ate enough of it to know how not to make a mess." He looked at her. "Maybe you could keep trying with the sauce."

Children, when they have erred, want to make things better. Mitch was calling attention, it is true, to his new mastery, but at Crissy's expense. He needed to know why that doesn't work with us in a way that he could repair the damage and go forth without fear.

The next time I served spaghetti, Crissy ordered "Spabetti, lots of sauce and cheese." Like Mitch, she was ready to "practice" until she got it right.

54

Who We Are Is the Good Parenting

ONE AFTERNOON FRANK stuck his head in the kitchen. "Hi," I said, wiping Crissy's face.

"You know what I'm thinking about doing? I'm thinking about using my law degree to work my way through art school. What do you think?"

I looked at the gleam in his eyes and said, "I think it's a great idea."

Danny ran by with Mitch in hot pursuit. Frank caught him and pulled him to him. Danny was four now and out of therapy. Dr. Dru doesn't think therapy should last more than a year for a very young child. If it does, you're in the wrong therapy, he says. "Come on, buddy, we're going home, go get your coat." As Dan ran off, Frank looked at me. "You know, I've wanted to be an artist since I was fourteen years old and my parents wouldn't consider it. They wanted a lawyer. It was none of their damn business but they didn't know that and neither did I." And he smiled. "Now I know it and

I'm taking responsibility for it. It wasn't their fault. I'm going to go to the art school."

I walked him to the door and stood there as he and Danny walked down the deck stairs.

I was glad Frank was going to go back to school to finally be what he always wanted to be—an artist, not an attorney. I felt certain that this was the best thing for his son Danny too.

As I walked back into the house and started cleaning up the playroom, putting each toy and book back in its place, I remembered a conversation that John, my son who's now thirty-three, and I had when he was twenty-two. At the time, I was just in the beginning years of my daycare and I was very excited. I had done this before in Kansas but not in my own place and I was learning things so much more quickly because I was in charge.

I had just learned how much children loved being read to so I was reading to them everything I could. It was so different from reading to my own kids—"Oh no—is that a long book or a short one? Let's get this over with."

When my eldest came into the kitchen while I was talking to Carol about how much I loved reading aloud, he said, "Gee, that must have been really wonderful for us."

I said, "When?"

"When we were growing up and stuff."

I blanched. "I didn't read to you guys."

John said, "What?"

"I hated reading when you were little."

"Gee, that really makes me feel bad, Mom. How can you read to all these kids and . . ."

"John, I was younger than you are right now when I had you. I was twenty years old."

"Oh my God," he said. "I was raised by a kid."

And he was.

*   *   *

As my own four children came into the world, they adjusted to me as I did to them. I am sure there is evidence of psychological damage in each, but today, I am not so narcissistic as I once was—I don't think I caused it all. The omnipotence that parents feel has been neutralized for me somewhat by doing this work. I am not quite so guilty about myself as a parent as I once was. But let one of my children just happen to casually say, "Mom, I just thought of something that you did. Do you remember the time when you . . ."

I gulp. I'm as afraid as the next parent of what my child is going to say.

Since I know as well as anybody what bad parenting is, it's much more interesting to ask, as I do with my daycare parents, what makes a good parent?

The answer surprises me as much as them. Like them, I thought good parenting was a special gift that only a few people had. Or the opposite, that it would come with children. But the truth is that what makes a good parent isn't so different from what makes a good *anything*.

A good parent is one whose life experience has basically been that they're effective. And that they're living pretty much the life they've chosen to live. It is the parent who has decided about him or herself, "I am a pretty good person in this world."

Secondly, a good parent is a person who is free of the kind of feelings that would cause them to live their lives through their children.

That vulnerability that we feel as parents and consequently the protective feelings that we have are all very natural. It is our baby's life that we hold in our hands and we would die for our child. Yet the irony of it all is that good parenting isn't in the holding on but in the letting go. We are tempted to keep them safe, but we can't.

The only time I really had any of my children, owned him or her, was in the womb. The moment my child was born was the moment we became two.

In that hospital room thirty-three years ago, when I held my first son John, I *knew* him. I knew that this was my baby and I would do anything for him—that moment was exactly the moment I had to let go. Birth is the first separation. I believe separation to be a lifelong issue between parent and child. And I also believe it proceeds well when parents understand that *this* is their life and *that* is their child's life.

We don't all have such clarity. But it is possible to leave to children, even very young ones, those decisions that are rightfully theirs. Each of us longs for evidence of our good parenting. With Frank's parents it was "my son the attorney." They believed so much that being a lawyer was the best one could be, so Frank came to believe it too.

I have found that the most painful times for me to let go of an expectation I held for one of my children's lives is when it represented some unfinished business in my own.

We don't have to teach them much either. What we value in life and the hopes we hold for them, we act out every day. What we have to give our children boils down to who we are. We can't fool them with our words—they know us in ways we don't even know ourselves. And who we are becomes the model for them.

I realized all this the day Frank came to tell me he was going to art school. I realized that the best that a parent can do is do the very best for themselves in their life. This will also help them not to hold on to their child so hard. They'll be too busy becoming everything that they can be.

55

Batwing Stew with Lizard Lips

ITCH, NOW WITH US TWO YEARS, swaggered into the kitchen, asking, "What's for lunch?"

"Batwing stew and cobweb bread," I said.

"Oh boy, I love batwing stew and cobweb bread." We continued to play this way for weeks.

"What's for lunch, Joanie?" he'd say each noon.

"Batwing stew and chicken lips, Mitch."

"Goody. I love that too. Ha ha ha."

Or sometimes when I'd say, "What do you want on your plate," he'd say, "I'll have cobweb bread and lizard tongue."

I'd say, "What we've got, Mitch, is hamburgers."

"Oh," he'd say. "Well, Joanie, I'll have hamburger and cheese, no bun."

We serve only what children ask for of the food we have

217

prepared. I've learned that children don't like foods mixed up. Casseroles, tuna salad, egg salad, and such are usually big disappointments. So we keep meat, vegetable, and starch separate. And because we're not pressured about what children choose to eat, mealtimes are relaxed times for us.

Children who choose what and how much, eat what they are served. And they are well behaved as they feel good about what they chose. Struggles about food are absent and we don't allow any other struggles at the table. The children don't have to eat the food but they don't get to throw it about or play with it either. They tell us when they are finished and we help them wipe their hands and mouths before they go back to play.

One day I had leftover stuffed grape leaves in the refrigerator and felt mischievous. Mitch came in and got washed up, and I served them to him after half the group had received baked chicken. I told him it was batwings stuffed with lizard lips, expecting him to be surprised and amused.

Instead, he said, "Oh . . ." hesitating. He didn't know what to do. But because he was Mitchell, he couldn't just say, "Oh, phewie, I never wanted that!" Instead, he looked up at me with those guileless blue eyes of his, and said, very seriously, "Thank you, Joan, for going to the trouble to get this for me. But you know, I really think I will have chicken today."

Immediately, I said, "They're really only stuffed grape leaves, Mitch. See," and I took a fork and opened one up for him. "I was trying to make a joke."

Looking back down at his plate, he said, graciously, "I see. Stuffed grape leaves. They do look fine but I think I'll stick with chicken, cut up and no skin, for lunch."

56

Meredith Changes
Her Family

J OAN," STEPHEN LAUGHED ONE DAY as he was picking
Meredith up after school. "Meredith is being so good
at dinner—" he got her coat, "we don't know what
to talk about anymore!"

Meredith, before she came here, was very hard on her
parents. Like a little princess, she ruled the roost. At dinnertime, it was all about Meredith: "Honey, don't throw your
food." She gulped her food down, barely able to breathe as
she gulped. "Where's the fire, baby?" her father would ask.

Her parents, Sandra and Stephen, spent the whole dinnertime in conversation, one way or another, involved with
moderating Meredith's behavior.

"Meredith, please come to the table."

"I like it where I am. I don't want to sit over there."

"Meredith, come to the table."
"But the sofa will miss me."

Then, after Meredith had been with us for a while, she began to change. First, she became more at ease, more directive about how she liked to spend her time. And her parents reported that Meredith wasn't bugging them while they were making dinner. Instead, she was in her room doing something.

When she came to the table, she said, "I'll have chicken, no skin and cut up, please. And just this much," she made a circle with her fingers, "salad, no dressing." She ate all of it, excused herself, happily wiped her own hands and face on a towel, and went back to her room to continue whatever she was doing. This change from a whining and needy person at dinner to a self-sufficient little person left a void. Her parents needed to find new ways to converse with Meredith.

I've learned over the years that as children make this place their own, they begin to change it, and then they begin to change. They do this by stating what else they need. "Joanie, I want apple raspberry juice." "Joanie? At my house we have blueberry pushups. Can we have blueberry pushups?" We have always shopped on this basis. Most of our toys have been bought to suit a particular individual—Wonder Horses for Joel and Derek, My Little Ponies for Jennifer and Tina, and so on. When a child says, "I want a Care Bear like in the movies," we respond by saying, "Well, I never thought of that," and we get two.

When it is okay to ask and get a direct nonjudgmental answer, children become very straightforward. They also become independent of us in their play, interacting with each other in a way that is more satisfying. They sometimes even choose to do things alone, reading or listening to cassette tapes.

This experience of managing one's own life successfully by one's own judgment and efforts creates an attitude about the self which allows the child to take the further risks he or she might need to grow.

However, parents may become fearful when their child's response to them is different. Like Meredith, the child comes home from his day intact, not needy or clinging to his parents as before, and instead goes to his room to play until he is called to dinner. The parent sometimes feels left out. "Where's Meredith?" they ask. Guilt may raise its ugly head. The parents then become susceptible to the punishing suspicion that new skills should rightfully be learned at home. Old ways of relating and communicating with the child are being outgrown, but new ones may be hard to accept because of the lurking resentful feeling that they are someone else's.

Consequently, Barbara and I need to stay connected to the parents. By that, I mean we must establish a good conversational relationship with them so that they remain informed of all that we can tell them about their child. They need to be included.

No, Meredith isn't becoming a stranger, she is only becoming more of who she is.

57

Kate and I
Part Company

Come on, little baby, we're going to the store," Jennifer said, pulling on Kate's, our play-drama teacher's, arm. It was a few months before she left for kindergarten and she had been working with Kate almost every time she came on the same theme.

Kate, playing the naughty baby once again, said, "Can I get some candy at the store, Mommy? Please, please, please?"

"No, you can't have any candy. You know I'm not going to buy you candy at the store. Now you just come on."

"But, Mommy," Kate whined. "I'm getting tired. I'm tired of walking. When will we be there? Pick me up. Carry me!"

"Quiet. Keep walking."

They went on and on like this. At the end of the story, Jennifer, the mother, always turned on her demanding baby to slap her and hit her, not really hurting Kate, of course, just ending the story with a spanking.

But Kate wanted Jennifer to turn and, instead of hitting her, feel compassion for the child. So one day, at the end of the story, instead of allowing her to beat on her, Kate stopped Jen's fist in midair with her hand and said, "Why do you hit me so much, Mommy, I'm just a little baby."

Jennifer put down her fist immediately and said, "That's not the story."

"That's right," I said, from the sofa. "It's not Jennifer's story, Kate."

"Oh, that's right," Kate said.

What happened with Kate, I think, is that she became impatient with the children's process—doing Jennifer's story over and over again, or Maggie's lizard, or doing Sara's Cinderella among the stepsisters. She came to believe she could be more effective sooner if she intervened.

During Kate's later years here, she went back to school to become a psychologist. This last year she had started her own therapeutic practice. And I watched her become increasingly impatient with allowing children the freedom they needed to play out their fantasies.

Finally, she said, "Joan, I don't have the energy I used to have. When I am getting ready to come here I feel so tired."

She missed a couple of times, calling to say, "I'm not going to come this morning," which was something she could do with us. Then a month went by and she hadn't called. Barbara called her and she said, "I'm getting so busy with my practice, I just don't seem to have the time for working with the children at your place. I'm exhausted by doing it." And, of course, Barbara and I accepted that. A few days later, Kate came by and said good-bye to the children.

I think what finally exhausted Kate was that she began to have a goal in her work with the children here. Who she was as therapist was getting mixed up with who she was in daycare. Therapists do intervene, have goals, and measure progress.

This therapeutic expectation was very different from our expectation of her. We looked to Kate to structure the dramatization of children's stories. She was a facilitator who saw to it that each child was allowed the time and attention needed to express his or her self. Then she was to oversee the participation of others in acting the story out.

It was crucial that each detail told by the child be remembered, and included, in order in the dramatization. Over time the details, often conflicting and not making sense on the whole, became transformed as the child acted them out so that an organized piece was presented with a beginning, middle, and end. This took many weeks but once it was accomplished the story was no longer of interest to the child and another one would begin.

When these were Kate's expectations of herself, she played a valuable role here. To the children she was "just playing" with them. She could be trusted to go along with whatever they had in mind. She ate babies, killed benign beings, and was very naughty whenever she was called upon.

Her value to me was that she was able to do what I could not. I am the caretaker, she the playmate. In these dramas each child showed me parts of themselves I would not otherwise see. A child telling "what is on his mind" is more direct and illuminating than what I can observe in his play in the other part of the day. Play-drama is also more direct "play" for the child too, for it helps him make sense out of what's on his mind. It is his own play that he writes, directs, and casts. The details of a painful trip to the store, for instance, change in the countless retelling until he can manage his feelings.

Kate, by her involvement, gave permission to express these feelings by the child. She and the other children all together working on his or her story become a powerful vehicle to support him in his efforts to maintain a steady course in a world he cannot yet fully understand, a world that he can only *experience* in these early years.

In this play-drama, the child is able to change his or her perception of an experience until it no longer disturbs him. He or she is the wizard in the magic kingdom who waves a wand, turning evil into goodness, a spanking into love taps, hateful feelings into lovely ones. The force toward goodness and harmony is great in all of us. Play-drama allows the child yet another way to slay the dragons that stand in the way of his releasing his own goodness.

Except for Jason. We needed another kind of magic for this little boy.

58

Jason Comes into My Life

WHO IS THIS CHILD, bare-assed, running on tip-toes?'' my friend Carol said as she walked in the deck gate as Jason and I were watering the geraniums. I had just bodily removed him from the group because he was a propeller of churning energy—constantly running into things, dumping toys, smashing and hitting the others.

"Do you remember that dinner party? Oh, $2\frac{1}{2}$ years ago? When Charleton told me about that boy born to his mother in a coma? Well, this is the one.'' He had come to us with terrible diarrhea and a bad cold. He also had a green dripping nose I was always wiping in spite of his efforts to push me away. And he had a bad diaper rash, which was why he was running around in the sun wearing only his Superman T-shirt.

Carol and I sat down when my eighteen-year-old daughter Karen, who was helping out now, came and got Jason for snacktime.

When Jason was two years old, his father, Scott, found out about us and came in for an interview. When he said over the phone that his wife was ill and had been institutionalized because she had had an accident to the brain, I thought that he meant an automobile accident. It didn't occur to me that Jason was the baby Charleton had told me about.

And so Jason and his father came in for the interview.

He was all over the playroom. He'd dump out a box of blocks and then dump out a carton of dolls. At this point he was two years and two months old and he would sc-*cream* at the top of his lungs. Scott would stop talking to Barbara and me, look over at his son, and say, "Oh, you want me to get down the red car for you?" I asked about the screaming. Scott said, "His mother screams a lot. He copies her."

His father had gotten so used to his screaming that I don't think he realized how shrill it was. He kept on talking about Jason coming and we answered questions about our methods. A child was leaving so we actually had space before September, which was unusual.

Between our interview and when Jason actually started with us, I realized, This is the child. I called Scott and said that I knew Charleton and that he had told me about Jason before he was born. Scott was thrilled because he loved Charleton. Then he told me the rest of the story.

At nine months, after his mother had been in a coma for the last five of them, labor began. Jason was born in four hours, without any voluntary muscle control on his mother's part. It was an easy labor; the only apparent difference in the baby was that he was born a little thin.

They put him to her breast, hoping that the feel of the baby would urge her to produce milk. But it didn't.

On the fourth day, as they once again put him to her breast, she woke up. And she looked down at Jason and then up at the nurse and said, "What happened? Where have I been?" Then she slipped back into a coma.

This went on and on. She would be there, but then disappear.

Jason was taken to and from the hospital in an attempt to bond them. But she was too erratic. They were trying to bond this baby to a person who was brain damaged.

Fortunately, Scott's relatives were people of means and even though Scott was a welder and had no personal resources, his relatives gave all their financial as well as emotional support to the mother. They took her from one place to another. During this time, Jason was cared for by one of his mother's caretakers, which was very difficult since the mother needed so much attention. For fourteen months they continued to try to manage baby and mother together until the mother was well.

His mother would have screaming episodes. If the person who was attending her was changing Jason's diaper, she'd scream, "Don't take care of him, take care of me! What are you doing?" Yet at other times, she'd yell at them, "My child! He's crying! Why don't you take care of my child?"

Of course, hindsight is always clearer. And what was lost in these months of crisis with the mother and the constant search for what could make her well was Jason. Scott believed at that time that his wife Janet would recover. And he believed that Jason and Janet would be close because they were never separated. However, later it seemed clear that a caretaker for Jason, separate from one caring for the needs of the mother, could have offered the one-to-one caring in his mother's absence that Jason needed.

After these fourteen months and no improvement, her family discovered a hospital for her in Europe that was doing wonders for persons with aneurysms. But they sent her back home after only four weeks. They couldn't help her. And on the plane back, she had another aneurysm. After this one, it was clear there was nothing more to be done. A year later, while Jason was with us, she died of a third and final aneurysm. She was thirty-eight years old.

When I finished that story, Carol looked over at me and said, "So, you have another interesting one. Are you up to it?"

I smiled. Carol and I had been so busy over the last few years that we didn't visit as often as I'd like. "You know, I'm really grateful for all the help you gave me with Timmy D. and Jeffie," I said. "You really were my first supervisor."

"No, I wasn't," she said. "I put that off on Rolph."

"Rolph," I sighed. "No. You made me feel adequate and so I could be open enough to listen. With Rolph, I always felt I wasn't enough, that he knew more than I did."

"Dr. Dru seems to really work for you, huh?" She got up off the deck chair to go into the house.

"He *really* works for the parents and the child who needs him." I smiled as I got up too. "With him I feel like a peer. It's not *my* therapy—it's supervision about the troubles of the child."

As she started to go in the front door, Carol turned, her shiny earrings catching the light, as she said, "Is Jason always on tiptoes?"

"I don't know," I said. "I haven't really noticed that about him. I'll pay attention."

"My experience has been that when a child walks continually on his toptoes, it might be an indication of a neurological problem."

I looked at her in dismay. "Another problem?" I shook my head. "Doesn't this little boy have enough already?"

59

An Unusual Bottle Schedule

DRU FOUND NO NEUROLOGICAL DAMAGE with Jason at this point, but he pointed out to me from the very beginning that because of the nature of his early care Jason never bonded with his mother, and consequently, there was no humbling, tempering separation. Prior to Jason's coming to our daycare, Dru had been counseling the family, and by this time, was working directly with Jason in therapy.

He came over for coffee one naptime with a feeding plan. Since bonding had not occurred because the mother was not present, and since there was no substitute for her in Jason's infancy, Dru wanted to put Jason on a rather unusual bottle schedule. We were to give him a bottle like clockwork every three hours and any other times he chose to have one also. And every time we gave him a bottle we were to hold and rock him.

He decided he was in love with Karen, my eldest daughter. Jason was in constant search for a mother. I let her be in charge of him. In this way, we offered the possibility to Jason of forming an attachment to her. Then when the time came to wean him from the bottle—that is, Karen—Jason would experience a gradual separation from her. If this really happened we'd perhaps see a tempering of the narcissism and omnipotence that characterized his personality.

At our daycare, we were always dealing with Jason's "me first, me only, *mine*" attitude. We hadn't found a way to make his expectations realistic. We had to be so heavy-handed with him that I was constantly counseling with Dru. "Don't worry about his ego, Joan. He is full of omnipotent feelings. Be as hard on him as you need to be. He needs to know that you are in charge, that you are bigger, older, and wiser than he, and he must succumb to that."

We'd see Karen every three hours running after this wild boy with a bottle. He'd stop, grab it, and run. "Jason!" she'd call. "Come here, I'll hold you!" That's the last thing he wanted.

"JASON! JASON! I'm just going to hold you—no, don't! Jason! Stop it!"

It was like trying to hold a whirling dervish.

At first, Karen, quite swept away with Jason's need for her, tried relentlessly to keep the schedule, but Jason would not be held.

Instead he was all over the place. And, in fact, he had found a cohort in crime, another wild boy, Barney, who had severe allergy problems and was also very high-strung. The two of them would run up and down the playroom and outside, *screaming* at the top of their lungs. In five minutes, they had the uncanny ability to stomp, break, hurt, and *devastate* anything in their way.

Dr. Dru said to me, "Joan, it would mean so much if you can civilize this kid . . . I'll help you do it. I know you can do it."

I believed I could do it too.

*   *   *

Jason and Barney became a great pair. When they connected it was like the slap of a hand! Sparks would fly. Each day they ran screaming from one end of the play yard to the other, knocking over kids, bikes, throwing sand at each other and everyone else, climbing up and down the stairs, throwing apple cores.

I was exhausted every night with both of them. With Jason I knew that my disapproval didn't count. It didn't really matter to him how any of us felt toward him. And with Barney, who was so hyperactive that he simply didn't know how to rest, I was at my wit's end.

I finally called Dr. Dru from daycare. "I have no energy left. There are ten other children here under the age of five and Jason is equal to all eleven, except Barney."

Actually, I felt sympathetic toward Barney. He was allergic to most foods—wheat, eggs, milk and milk products, some food dyes, and many food preservatives. These allergies made him so agitated that, not only was he difficult to control, but he couldn't sleep. His mother said that it was as if he had an automatic washer churning inside him all the time. Yet, I actually felt we were making headway with him. His mother was researching allergies and sharing all her information with us. We were careful to only serve him his special foods. And Barney was responding.

But Jason?

I guess Dr. Dru heard the desperation in my voice. He lived only a few blocks away and he said he'd get on his homemade motorized bike and zip right over. It was drizzling outside, so he held an umbrella over his head with one hand as he pedaled electrically down the street and up the driveway.

Meanwhile, Jason and Barney were running up and down the playroom throwing a Nerf ball at each other, slapping their feet on the other children's puzzles, books, and toys as they played. Because the weather was nasty, we were all inside near the fire. I was sitting in my place on the floor trying to read with Meredith and the rest of the five little girls. Karen was running after Jason, trying to catch him once again to give him a bottle. He'd already hit me, Barbara, and two other children.

Dru walked in the door, took off his frayed raincoat, and stood in the playroom doorway. He held out his arm and with the other hand hit a tiny chime on his watch. *Pringgg.*

Jason stopped in midflight, turned, and stared.

"Hi, Joanie," Dru said, ignoring Jason. He went over to the sofa and sat down, and Jason dropped his ball and listened. *Pringgg.*

Dru sometimes doesn't seem to be in his body at all— just all eyes. He didn't move to invite Jason over. Jason was spellbound as he came over to Dru. And a tiny gold chime sounded.

Jason stood beside him, Dru gently picked up Jason's arm. "See?" he said and pushed Jason's index finger down on a button on his watch. *Buzzzz. Pringgg.*

Jason laughed delightedly, put his other hand gently on Dru's shoulder, and leaned closer to him to see the watch better.

I wanted Dru to observe and advise and see what it was we were dealing with every day. Yet when he arrives, this little angel comes over and looks at his watch.

All Dru would say was, "Okay, now, listen . . ." and the seconds would go by and I, of course, could not believe it. I had never seen this little terror so silent, let alone transfixed. Then there would be this tiny chime and buzzer and Jason would get all excited. And he settled down.

Afterward, I said to him, "Dru, obviously I don't have the same kind of magic that you have with Jason."

"It's the relationship, Joan. You see him in the real world. The therapeutic relationship is different." Then I described to him once again, since Jason certainly wouldn't, his behavior and my futile attempts to moderate it. He was very patient with me that day and listened gently to all my concerns. And with his help, I began to learn about managing aggression. Or, I should say, I learned about "coming up to" aggression.

One day, when Jason started screaming, I grabbed his face and I screamed too. He understood that. And he actually stopped screaming. It was all right with him. Prior to this time, he would scream for long periods of time for no apparent reason. I would try to get his attention and tell him to stop screaming and carry him about. But he always continued screaming until he stopped of his own accord.

Now when he'd be frantically racing around, I would grab him, pick him up, hold him, and yell, "STOP RUNNING AROUND!"

He'd quiet down in my arms, then put his feet down and run off. He responded to these gestapo kinds of tactics. At first it felt cruel to me, but gradually I began to really understand what I was doing. This is the support he needed. And he became generally calmer when I used this approach. But he was still very difficult to care for all day.

At least I had Dru to call. He always said to me, "Yes, it is very very difficult, Joan, and you know, you don't have to do it." So I chose it each time. And this made a difference.

I also taught Karen to come up to Jason's aggression. What Dru was after with the bottle schedule was to set up some kind of rhythm that we could then wean Jason away from. If Jason began to feel comfortable being held and rocked when he drank his bottle, then we had something finally that we could take away. Perhaps *that* would matter.

60

Adversity

WHEN I FINALLY HAD TIME to take it all in, I realized how done in I was by Jason and Barney. There was a small part of me that simply wanted to stop what I was doing and find something easier. Yet the larger part of me knew this is where I belonged.

My whole being and heritage was about being able to deal with adversity. In fact, I didn't have a close friend who hadn't come from great difficulty. Above all, my ability to find strength in the midst of turmoil was a direct result of my parenting. My mother and father came out of great adversity and as best they could, made something wonderful out of it.

My mother was a wonderful woman from country people who made her world beautiful even in the midst of tremendous difficulty. Although it was painful for her, I think she had a healthy childhood in the sense that she wasn't confused by it, she knew what was going on and could make some change. I think that's what matters. Children who grow up in the most horrible circumstances can survive it if there's some organization, some continuity. Mother survived her hard situation and it actually gave her a real feeling of peace with what she had. Even during those times when my father was heartbroken and drinking, I remember my mother as a very peaceful, content person.

I can just see her sitting down and taking stock at the end of the day, rocking in her rocker. "Well, you know we have food in the cupboards, Dad's employed, Joanie's safe in bed, and I'm going to darn these socks, I'm going to make a braided rug, and tomorrow I'll do the garden."

My mother loved elegant, simple things. She knew how to cook wild game. She loved baking bread. My father enjoyed entertaining because my mother presented such a festive, unique, almost magical table. I remember going out to dinner once with my family and noticing that all the plate and glasses matched and I thought it was boring. My mother got her plates, each one different, from what she called the "not new" shops, and the silverware never matched. She crocheted her own tablecloths and our food was from the garden. This was a time after the war when people went out of their way to have store-bought food.

When I think for myself what gives me peace in the midst of such a hectic and demanding life, it is that I have inherited my mother's love of harmony, order, and beauty. Like my mother, I am always changing things to make them beautiful.

She grew up in Elroy, Wisconsin. Her father was a barber and he owned his own shop. He was also an influential man in town, an alderman. Then he started drinking and became the town drunk. Their house burned down, he lost his shop, and he left his family for a time. In desperation, my grandmother took in other people's laundry. My mother had four other brothers and sisters. One morning she woke up and her homemade feather comforter was covered with snow. The wind had blown it in through the cracks in the wall. She got up and started taking off layers upon layers of clothes to get dressed, because that's the only way she could stay warm in bed. Her leather boots had frozen stiff so her fingers became raw with trying to pull the buttons through with the button hook. When she went downstairs Grandma was sitting in her rocker. She hadn't lit a fire, or made coffee, or anything. She stayed in that rocker for nine months. They would feed her and every once in a while she would wander. In nice weather she would sit and watch the chickens out in the yard. They went and found their father and told him that there was something wrong with her. He came home and started working part-time in the barber shop he had sold. He stayed sober, bringing them food and coal. Then nine months later, my mother got up one morning and smelled coffee. She thought maybe her older sister was making it. But when she went downstairs, there was Grandma, busy in the kitchen. She just took up where she left off.

And somehow, during all this, my mother learned to stay in balance by contenting herself with a plan for creating something lovely, however small. My dad, on the other hand, wasn't very content. He was from Garrison, South Dakota, of Norwegian stock, and he was always trying to better himself. Yet, despite it all, he was a very nurturing man, very understanding. Dr. Dru reminds me a bit of my father. I'd be so upset about something and he'd smile and give me some real words of wisdom.

I think a lot of my feeling very secure about my own self and my own efforts and what I can do comes from my father's acceptance and philosophical point of view about life. "Joanie," he'd say, "don't be so surprised. Life is hard."

One of the things that parents need to let their children know is that life is difficult. You don't need to sit and lecture, but there's a way of not being surprised about problems and there's a way of not being upset about them too. It's a way of being a model for working things through. "Sure, it is difficult, but this is what we can do about it." This kind of nonhysterical stance about it makes you realize that you're neither so omnipotent that you can control everything nor so powerless that you're a victim of circumstance. I learned this from my father. He was good at that middle road, the moderated path.

Besides my father's gentle realism, I received just pure love from my mother, who was so innocent and so naive about the world. She met my father at a dance when he played his trombone during the summer. When he asked her to marry him she was afraid to say yes for fear that she would be abducted by white slavers when she took the train to Washington where he lived. And while this naiveté infuriated me sometimes, what she did have was great contentment and very strong feelings of love. She was a wonderful teacher. She knew people learned by fits and starts—two steps forward, one step back. There was always permission with my mother to do your best without fear, which brings out the best in everyone. Mistakes were not only okay but necessary, that's the way it works. And she loved her children.

I remember giving her such adversity. When she was pregnant with my younger sister, Linda, who is eighteen years younger than me, I was giving her a permanent. The baby was due in three weeks when my mother started to get contractions and she said to me, "Joanie, I think my water just broke. I'm wet."

I said, "Let's get this permanent done then."

"Joanie, get these curlers out of my hair."

"Mom, it takes you twenty hours to have a baby."

"Joanie! Get these curlers out of my hair!"

61

The Art of Naptime

URING THIS TIME, my younger sister Linda decided to start her own daycare and Barbara offered to go work with her for a week. She and I planned feverishly so that there would be a smooth transition for the children and their parents. A week doesn't really seem like a long time but changes are always difficult for young children. Just as Meredith found it hard to say good-bye to trash, it would be hard for the children to even briefly do without Barbara. Consistency is the key. We even prepare them for details such as a new sofa in the playroom. We tell them about it, showing them on the calendar the day when it will arrive and the old one will go. Consequently, we carefully prepared them for Barbara's absence.

Only—funny thing—I forgot to prepare myself. On the Sunday night before the day, I couldn't fall asleep because something was on my mind. The only problem was, I couldn't quite figure out what was bothering me. Monday morning came. It was supposed to be exciting. Barbara was off and my daughter Karen was going to be my partner all alone for the week. As each child arrived, they said, "Hi, Joanie! Hi, Karen! Where's Barbara?"

"Remember, Ana, Barbara is away for a week?"

"Where'd she go?"

"What she doing?"

I reminded them about where Barbara was and what she was doing and then Karen talked about all the exciting things we were going to do. Cook, shop for groceries, and one nap-time Karen would take some of them to the zoo instead of nap. If it was all so interesting, why was I so depressed?

It came to me about 10:30 that morning: I missed her. So I did the natural thing and called her up. But she sounded so great that I didn't share my own feelings. We just chatted about unimportant things. I was glad that I called her, though, because now I felt a bit angry. When I missed her the rest of the day it helped having a bit of anger toward her. I saw her that night. She was bubbling over with enthusiasm for Linda's place and how much fun they were having.

"Do you think a week is long enough to help?" I asked.

"Oh yeah, it's more than enough and I'm okay doing it."

I looked at her, feeling like it was not okay for me and that the four days left seemed a long time.

Around 10:00 A.M. the next day I could tell I was mad at Barbara for not being there. But why? I asked myself. As I tried to identify what was the matter, I realized that for all day yesterday and the first two hours of today I had not been able to show my impatience toward a child. For instance, I was feeling impatient with Barney, as usual, who for the last thirty minutes was either banging into me, or pulling on me, or rocking against me. I wanted to get away from this per-petual motion machine for ten minutes. If Barbara were here I could have walked away and not even looked back because she always noticed and would take up immediately where I left off. In fact, if she were here I wouldn't even have had to give myself a time limit of ten minutes. I wouldn't have thought in terms of coming or not coming back at all; I would have been free.

This isn't to say that I couldn't reach out to my daughter to take my place. I could have told her that I needed to get away and she would have done what she does so well for a child. To do all this simple arranging, though, seemed too demanding, so I sat with Barney, continuing to purposefully separate him from Jason.

Does Barbara read my mind? I wondered. She must. I never have to ask, explain, or say any words to make my actions clear to either of us. She just knows.

At lunchtime, I felt stifled and again I asked myself why. If Barbara were here, I realized I could have yelled at Jason the third time he demanded rudely to be served the spaghetti that was still softening in the boiling water, instead of trying at his fifth rude demand to "make things okay" for him that lunch was late.

Most of all, I realized a part of me was missing—the Barbara part—the part that lets me know I can trust my own spontaneous reactions to children. Barbara would never let me verbally abuse a child. She better come back soon, I thought, or I may let loose with this one. But I laughed to myself for I understood what all this was about. If I didn't let my feelings out, I was going to have an ulcer or give a child a bloody nose. When I am with Barbara I can just be me. The two of us are enough.

Feeling absolutely frustrated, angry, and sorry for my-self, I cleaned up the kitchen as Karen took the children to nap. This is Barbara's job. She has always managed naptime from the day we started working together. Naptime for her is twelve little bodies sleeping on twelve little cots, cozy with their assortment of books, cuddly toys, and blankets. Naptime for Karen that day was twelve little bodies going wild in the main playroom, crawling over and under the cots, throwing things, some reading—it was true—but Jason and Barney throwing their cuddly toys at each other and screaming.

When I walked into the playroom that day, Ana was standing on her cot, her pants down, showing everyone her 'litteris. I have never seen a little girl who loved her vagina more. I just stood in the doorway and looked at her and then at the rest of the kids. Children crowded around me. "Joanie, can I?" "He hit me. He hit me!" "No, I did not." Karen said to me, "Where's the—" as she set up the last few cots. "Whose sock is that?" I said as one flew through the air and hit the wall. "Jason! If you don't—"

It was then that I remembered Barbara had left me a list of instructions. Just yesterday I had stuffed them arrogantly into a drawer. I didn't need instructions. Now I ran to the hutch in the other room to find them. When I returned, believe me, I followed them to the letter.

Dear Joan,

  1. Take the phone off the hook.
  2. Ask each child to show you which cot he or she sleeps on (Barbara knew that even with a map I'd never get it right). Put Bev and Christopher in cribs.
  3. Ask toilet trained children if they need to pee. If they say, "No," you are to ask them to "go to the toilet and see if pee will come out."
  4. As you ask about the toilet, go around the room and remove shoes, asking about removing socks. (Some prefer to sleep with their socks, it seems. None in the current group need to sleep with their shoes on, so don't bring that up as a possibility.)
  5. Make two milk bottles and two apple juice bottles and warm Barney's soya milk formula by adding hot water from the tap to the refrigerated three ounces of soya concentrate that is in a bottle on the refrigerator door shelf. Sally and Jason get the milk bottles. Mary and Nate accept only apple juice.

6. *Before* you prepare the bottles and *after* the children are settled (toileted, shoes off, and covered up) put on the *Fox and Hound* record on low volume #3.

7. Give those who use them their bottles and ask aloud to the group if they are all set. If they are not, do as they ask to settle them. Bramble hates what she calls "squishy pillows." If she's unhappy see if she took the wrong pillow and let her exchange it for a "nonsquishy" one as she doesn't like it to be called a "hard" one. We know the opposite of squishy is harder or firmer, but she won't accept another pillow if it's been called either hard or firm. So if she looks unhappy ask about the exchange as she may not want to tell you that that's what it is about.

8. Now lie down between Joel and Derek's cribs. Pat Joel on his back softly while looking into Derek's eyes. Derek will lie still and go to sleep quickly if you keep eye contact with him. If you lose it he'll get up. Lie him back down and soberly tell him to go to sleep (*don't* smile) and keep watching his eyes until they close. Once they are closed, keep watching as he sometimes is only testing you and they'll pop open again. He is really sleeping when he is breathing regularly and is not sucking his fingers rhythmically.

9. Mary has learned that I need to put these two to sleep before I can tend to her. Remember that she is waiting for you to lie beside her once these two are asleep and don't skip doing this even if she is snoozing because she'll know if you did it or not and if you didn't she'll wake up at 2:00 and cry because you forgot her. If she's awake just lie beside her but don't touch or pat her. She hates that. Stay there till she sleeps. If she's sleeping lie down beside her anyway for *at least five minutes.* Take my word on this one, Joan. If you don't, she'll be brokenhearted and if that's not enough to keep you there remember that when

her heart is broken she cries *very loudly* and *for a very long time* and EVERYONE WAKES UP!

10. It should be about 1:15 by now if all has gone well. Look about. If anyone is still awake lie next to them *but* don't talk to them, touch them, or in any way make eye contact. You don't want to communicate anything that they may want to respond to in the way of conversation. Your nonverbal message must continually be: go to sleep . . . go to sleep. To get this to happen you must think it over and over in your mind. You are there but not available. Got it? Now that everyone is sleeping you can lie on the couch and sleep too. You'll need it.

Love, Barbara

At 2:00 P.M., only forty-five minutes behind her schedule, all the children were sleeping. Barbara's instructions were perfect. As I watched these sleeping little ones that I had put down with Barbara's love and caring, I marveled yet again at the depth of this well that is Barbara's love.

I walked over to the bookcase for a magazine to read on the couch when Bramble began to stir. This wasn't in the plan. I quickly pulled a cot over to hers and laid down next to her, hoping that this would be enough to send her back, although to be frank, I had visions of twelve children waking up and crying around me. Where are you, Barbara?

62

Little Steelgod

BARBARA SAID TO ME, "When I feel less sympathy for a child, you are always more sympathetic."

I laughed. "That's so true. And when I get angry you always become kinder."

Throughout the next three days I continued to feel the absence of Barbara, but not in a way that perhaps someone else might fill. Karen and I were quite capable of caring for these children; in fact, the group was good with she and I working together.

The fourth evening, Barbara came over and I finally had an opportunity to talk to her about what I was feeling. After listening to my clumsy efforts, she said, "It sounds like the same feelings you had when you and your husband divorced!" We laughed at this and I felt lighter. I am so glad my sister and I are partners in work, not in marriage!

As it turns out, Barbara missed me terribly too. We decided we were fortunate to have this opportunity to learn that in our work we are one individual.

I picture a container that we both keep full. I don't know who contributes the most. What's important for our children and our work is that generally it remains full.

This fact was brought home to me even more strongly two weeks after Barbara returned.

It was spring now and very beautiful. Most of the children were down in the play yard on the swings with Barbara. I happened to be showing two new daycare parents around. We were walking on the deck and I was saying, "Yes, we have two swings, a sand box, that's a basketball net . . ."

The kitchen door was opened out to the deck. Karen, who continued to deal with Jason, was holding him on the dining table with a bottle in her hand while screaming, "STOP IT! STOP IT!" at the top of her lungs. And Jason was screaming back at her, his mouth huge, his handsome curly hair damp with exertion, "*STOP IT!*" She was simply doing what she had been taught to—meeting his aggression full on.

However, the sound of her "STOP IT! STOP IT!" came out the kitchen door as the parents and I walked by. "*STOP IT!*" a little boy's voice screamed furiously back.

"You're probably wondering what's going on," I said with a smile at the parents.

"Is that a playhouse over there?" the mother said, ignoring me and beginning to walk toward it. She turned, and said, "From your reputation, Joan, I am quite sure you know what you're doing."

Really, I thought to myself, if she only knew.

Finally, he stopped screaming, but Karen had reached a point with Jason where she could no longer stand it.

He was a handsome child, seductive really. You wanted to hold him and play with him and delight in his bright green eyes and his shiny black curly hair. But he had little tolerance for anyone but himself. He longed for intimacy. But he drained those around him. "Me, me, me" were what his actions were about. Once he'd seduce you, he'd drop you and go find someone else. He'd be quite docile at first, quite interested, almost fun, but then when you were there with him, he wore you out with his constant demands.

Karen finally came to me depleted and said that she wanted to quit childcare because she was terrible at her job. "Mom, I just don't have it," she said. "I'm not meant to work with kids."

"Karen," I sat her down at the kitchen table, "I've watched you. You're wonderful with children. It's Jason, not you." And I said aloud what I had been thinking for some time. "Enough is enough. I don't want to deal with him either."

Barbara came into the kitchen to get a Pepsi from the refrigerator. She said, "I will."

"You will what?" I said.

"*I'll* deal with Jason from now on." She came over and sat by us at the round kitchen table.

"Fine," I said. "But you're going to have to deal with everybody else too, because I am not working all by myself and Jason is a *full-time job*."

"I can do Jason and I can do my job," she said.

So Karen and I both said, "Okay, fine."

So Barbara began. She was the one now to discipline him, give him the bottle, and try to give him comfort. It was very hard for him to accept any tenderness at all. It was amazing that he switched to Barbara so readily. It meant Karen's dedication didn't get in. Little steelgod, he was very very hard. It never felt like anything could seep in.

Later, I said to Dru, "We can't continue this bottle schedule. It's doing more harm than good. It's like trying to pull a monkey's hands off a bar."

And he said what he always said. "Joan, if it isn't working for you, don't do it." And so we stopped.

63

I Teach a Child
to Sleep

UT I WILL BE LONELY.''

"You won't be alone," I said. "I will stay with you the whole time, even when you are asleep."

"But I don't like it upstairs," Barney said. "I want to be downstairs with Barbara and the kids. I don't like you."

"Let's go upstairs and I'll show you our room."

Barney was a child who couldn't sleep. By $2\frac{1}{2}$ years of age, most of those foods and additives that he was allergic to had been discovered. This had been a long process and we were still finding other substances, even a year later, that had to be removed from his diet. As a result, he was sometimes still a jumping bean inside. He never had a restful nap or awakened refreshed from a night of real sleep. His timetable

248

was such that he actually only napped for maybe twenty-minute periods on and off throughout a twenty-four-hour day. No matter how good Barbara was at the art of naptime, Barney never slept for more than twenty minutes.

So, of course, he hated going into naptime for he knew he wouldn't be able to do it. He would gather all his nap things like the other nappers and go in but he was defeated before he began. He would drink a bottle, fall asleep, then twenty minutes later, he was awake and energized, ready to go. It was cruel to expect him to lie quietly for another hour and forty minutes.

And it never worked. On those days when he was obviously reacting to something in his system (even some medications overstimulated him and had to be phased out), he couldn't sleep at all. However, as time went on, there were more days when he was calm and apparently sleepy, in need of rest that wouldn't come. By the end of each day he was miserable with tiredness. His mother always came for him at four. Even this shorter day was too difficult without more rest. Together she and I decided that somehow Barney needed to sleep two hours from one to three like everyone else. So I asked Karen to take my place with the five older girls who now went without naps and I went upstairs to teach Barney how to sleep.

"This is my room, Barney. This is where I sleep at night." I then showed him the closet.

"Why do you keep your vacuum sweeper in here?"

"I keep it here because it is big closet and there is room for it here."

"Do you have two vacuums?" he asked.

"Yes, I have one downstairs too."

"We do too."

"Ah," I said. "We have the same."

"I like mine better. Yours looks funny."

I smiled. "Would you like to see where Karen and Laura sleep?"

"No."

"Would you like to see the bathroom?"

"Yes."

We saw the bathroom and then I said, "I want to show you where you and I will nap today."

"It's dark in here."

"I'll open the shades. Now it is light. Look around."

He did. "Who sleeps here?" he asked.

"No one right now. It was Tim's room before he went away to college."

Barney felt strange up here; nothing was familiar. Even the vacuums were odd. I said, "You feel uncomfortable because this is all new. You can find something you would like to bring up here from the playroom. Maybe you'd like to bring several things. See, I have put your own pillow and blanket from your house in the crib."

He looked more closely at his sleeping place. Then I lowered the shades again and we left the room.

After lunch he told me that he was going to sleep with Babar. Babar, the King of the Elephants, was a stuffed small gray character with green pants and a coat that came on and off. He had a yellow crown made of felt that was glued to the top of his head. Babar was the only toy Barney chose to keep him company.

Since he slept in a crib at home, I chose a crib, not a cot for him. When we got upstairs, I took off his shoes and lifted him into the crib. I covered him and gave him his bottle. He held Babar close to his cheek and fell asleep before his bottle was empty, while I sat comfortably in an easy chair where he could see me. I looked away from him, deliberately not making eye contact. I was present but not available for conversation.

I sat there reading for a while, and then I began to wonder what it must feel like to be Barney. His mother described his allergic reaction as a washing machine agitator going inside him. While this was not how he felt today, it had been his constant sensation for months. When he woke twenty-five minutes later, I looked into his soft brown eyes and said, "Shh. Go back to sleep."

He had turned onto his stomach in his sleep. Clutching Babar in one arm, his bottle in his hand, he put his head down. I said, "Close your eyes." He tried. Squinted tightly shut and open, then shut and open. I moved toward him, still in my chair. I put my hand in his crib and started patting his back lightly and steadily. His eyes began to get heavier and heavier and he stopped squinting. He opened them every once in a while but was more relaxed. I continued to rub his back in circular motions, lightly and then more heavily if he looked wakeful. I felt him dozing on and off so I stopped. He immediately woke up.

I continued stroking him until he was wide awake and obviously had done all he could for one day. He had been in his crib for one hour when we came downstairs. After a month of this, he gradually was sleeping the entire naptime. He was sleeping at night now too. The twenty-minute sleeps had become a thing of the past. His sleep habits were changing.

64

Barney's Babar

B ARNEY DOESN'T WANT to bring Babar back, Joan, and I'm frankly hesitant to force him," his mother said to me on the phone. She was clearly worried about it.

"Yes," I said. "Babar has become so important to him." I was sitting upstairs in my room, gazing out the window at the birch trees.

Each afternoon Barney would go upstairs for his nap and trailing behind, bouncing on the stairs, held tightly in one hand was his beloved elephant, Babar. At the end of the day, he would be put back into the basket with all the other stuffed animals. The next day, someone else would get him out to play. Pretty soon Babar's crown would get all messed up and Barney would take him home so his mom could fix him and he'd bring it back. I could tell that Barney was pretty unhappy letting Babar into the care of the other children.

So I said to his mother, "You know, Babar is not treated this well by anybody else. I think that Barney should own Babar."

There was silence on the other end. Then she said, "How are you going to do that?"

"I'm simply going to tell anybody who cares that this is now Barney's Babar 'from his house.' "

She was worried that we were going to lose all our toys this way. But I explained, "The kids aren't like that. They very rarely form an attachment to the toys at our house. They know that everything belongs to everybody and so they're careful not to get overly attached. But," and I smiled to myself, "sometimes they fall in love."

The next day, Barney brought Babar back and I wrote BARNEY on Babar's tag. I said, "If anybody wants to play with this, you simply show them that this has your name on it and that it's 'yours from your house' because Joanie gave it to you. You can share it or not. That's the rule."

One specific and concrete way, beside directly giving a child a toy that they love, that we help children to see that there is "enough" for each of them is to equip our playroom with an abundance of toys, games, books, dolls, and any other equipment that is enjoyable.

We belong to two book clubs and subscribe to two children's magazines beside monthly trips to bookstores. We purchase equipment often, either spontaneously or on planned trips, sometimes with a few children so that they can choose what we may overlook.

Rarely will we buy only one doll or one train. We know that children want to play together and that it's best if each is playing with a complete set. Though we may only need one more baby doll, we'll buy two so that we don't end up with only *one* new toy. It's easier to take turns with something new if there's more than one.

When *Star Wars'* figures were the rage and very difficult to get, we bought whatever we could in whatever quantity available. I remember the glee I felt when I brought into the playroom six of the ten favorite characters. But you see, we only had *one* Princess Leia, Chewbacca, Darth Vader, Han Solo, and Luke Skywalker—and half of the children wanted to be Luke and the other half wanted to be Darth Vader. It's very difficult to give up Darth to another knowing that one's turn will take a long time to come up again, since everybody else wants their turn too.

Terry had a simple solution for the frustration and pain of being without Darth. When his turn was over he accidentally on purpose pulled his leg off. Now no one wanted Darth Vader anymore, not even him.

Crissy asked me three times one hectic morning to please read Red Riding Hood. I was too busy at the time to sit down and read it to her. I knew she was struggling with something in the story because she had had me read it over and over again all week.

When I cleaned up at the end of the morning I found the Red Riding Hood book thrown in a corner. Several of its pages were torn out and one was crumpled up. I felt the anger in those torn pages and saw the tiny hand that became a fist crumpling the last page.

I burned the book in the fireplace to be rid of it and read to Crissy from a second copy (we must have half a dozen of them) as soon as she woke up from her nap.

What had bothered her (and also is troublesome for other children) was how could Red Riding Hood's mother send her alone through all those dark woods to Grandma's?

She said to me, "Do you think my mommy would do that?"

"No," I said, taking her in my arms.

*   *   *

Still, there was only one Babar.

The other children never had any trouble about it. They respected Babar's new owner. Then at five, just before Barney left us, he brought Babar back and said, "I don't want him anymore. He belongs here."

And so he does, but no one watches out for him the way Barney once did.

65

I Run into Steel

S O BARNEY *was* making progress. Regardless of our efforts, however, Jason seemed not to progress. He got bigger and older but changed little for the better. After a few months of Barbara's taking responsibility for him, I was even more willing to let Jason go. But Barbara said once again, "No, we're in this for the duration." And, the truth was, that every once in a while, we would have a little success with him that kept us hopeful.

Jason didn't let us comfort him when he got hurt. In fact, he rarely cried. I don't think he felt pain like you and I do. Little steelgod, he'd fall down and get up and go, often with the kind of gash that another child would cry over and need a Band-Aid. So whenever he fell hard enough to actually cry, I'd rush over to him and pick him up. Immediately, he'd want to get down. He was going to do it all by himself. I was frustrated. I wanted him to need someone.

Then one day, Barbara was in the house and he fell down and I picked him up.

You know how children kind of melt when you pick them up? They have a way of relaxing in your arms. Well, Jason never melted. He stayed hard; all angles. I never could find a soft place in this child.

So this one day he was really hurt and crying and I picked him up. And I said, "I'm going to hold you until you feel better."

He tried to scramble out of my arms but I said, "No, I'm going to hold you until you feel better."

By this time, I was walking around with him, repeating, "No, I'm just gonna hold you." And I kept saying that every time he tried to get down, as if it were some kind of odd little lullaby. "No, I'm just gonna, just gonna hold you . . . hold you." And he put his arms around my neck and his head on my shoulder and he just gave up.

And I thought, "Now we're getting somewhere."

Then one day, Barbara wasn't watching him for some reason, and Jason did about six things in a row that put the entire playground in turmoil. Upset, I ran over to him and grabbed him by the hair to pull him off Barney who was screaming. Still grasping him by the hair, I forced him into a sitting position on the ground.

I let go quickly. He was crying. I said, "I think I did that to get you to cry." And then I took him in my arms.

When he was comforted and Barbara came back into the yard, I set him down and walked away.

I told Karen where I was going and I walked through the large playroom and out the front door onto our front porch and I started numbly watering the geraniums and the water was going all over the place because I was trembling so hard.

I have never hurt a child.

Prior to this experience with Jason, I had believed that if I couldn't wholeheartedly accept a child this was not an emotionally healthy place for him or her to be. He or she needed to know they were safe in our care. And they always have been.

As far as I was concerned, the slate was always clean for a child. If not, if every time I looked at a child and I was thinking, "This kid is a biter," then I was surely holding that potential for him. It becomes an expectation. It is very difficult to have these judgments and help a child forward.

Children from two through four are not easy to be with. For one thing, they're always wet. They drool. Their hands are always in their mouths. One woman who used to help us out years ago had to quit because the children always wanted to touch her, and, in her words, "They are slimy."

I know that if you can't accept this runny nose, drooling, smelling of poop, nail-biting wet individual, then you shouldn't be working with this age child. Physically they're a mess. They pick their noses and eat their snot. They pick their sores and eat their scabs. They go outside and kill bugs by picking off their wings to notice how they negotiate without them. These behaviors don't really bother me. Because I value books, I care very much whether or not they chew on them. But on the whole, how they look or what they do with their fingers doesn't concern me.

But Jason was something else. And if there's something about a child that stood in my way from being able to pick him up and love him, then that became the unacceptable part of *him to him.*

And that was how I was feeling now, full of judgment, expectations, fear, loathing, and anger.

I had to tell Scott, his father, what I had done to Jason, and also Dru. I felt that if Jason had gotten all of what I was feeling at the moment I grabbed him by the hair, he had gotten too much. So when Scott came in to pick him up at the end of the day, I told him how I felt, that I was terribly angry at Jason for causing so much pain to the other children. "Scott, in six minutes he had four children crying, he had broken someone's toy, and he was in the process of pulling another toy away from someone else!" And I told him that I had grabbed Jason by the hair and sat him on the ground. "I think it was a big surprise and that it hurt. But I'm mostly concerned about my anger directed at him disturbing him."

Scott had had a lot of therapy by this time and he was open to my feelings about it. I wouldn't have said all that to most parents, but he and I had gone through so much together already that I was able to tell him the absolute truth. "Oh, Joan," he said. "I think it's probably fine, but if something comes of it, I'll tell you."

Then I called Dru and he said, "We all feel that way about him, Joan. He's so omnipotent, narcissistic, he never sees the other person." And then he said to me what he always says to me, "If this isn't for you, stop."

I felt horrible. I had had such hopes that we could help this little boy. My God, we had socialized every other child we had ever come in contact with, why not Jason? And I felt terrible all over again that I had grabbed him by the hair.

"I don't think your anger will make any difference to him," Dru said. "*But if it does it would be wonderful.* If Scott comes back to us and says that Jason had a nightmare over it or that he couldn't eat afterward . . . anything that would show that you had gotten through to him, that something had actually disturbed him."

But nothing happened, just him rampaging through the house and Barbara trying to help and Karen still trying to help, and me trying to keep the slate clean, and yet becoming increasingly discouraged.

66

Learning My Limitations

J ASON LEFT US IN SEPTEMBER of that year. My friend Carol turned out to be right about his walking on tiptoes. Just before he left us, at five, Dru did further testing, and it was true, he did have neurological damage. Though it was very slight, it allowed Jason to get into a very good kindergarten for special needs children.

A few days after he left, I was out on my front deck watering my geraniums, and I was thinking about my limitations. What were my limits with these children? Over the years, I've gone through terrible upsets sometimes seeing children I love go home with parents whom I felt didn't really understand or feel sympathetic to their problems. This wasn't true for Scott. What could I have done better to have helped Jason? Gone home with him? Would that have helped? And it wasn't just Jason. My quandary came down to this: what is the alternative? Raising the child myself? Away from his family? Hardly possible. And if it were, do I want to raise another child, and another? I don't. Then what is my commitment to these kids? And what I had come to, and what I still believe, is that my commitment is total to these kids while they are in my care, 9 to 5, from two to four.

But what about Jason? I thought to myself as I watered. What did I learn? For one, a lesson in aggression. I learned I must rise to the level of aggression of the child. Sometimes I feel like a seesaw, up and down; it takes a lot to rise up one more time to physically restrain a child when a simple "don't" would be enough for another. Today I can summon the aggression I need to do that and still feel like a good person, for the intention is always to protect the child.

You know, on the other hand, I don't think we made much of a dent in Jason's personality like we have with so many other children. But I know he made one in mine. And I think I learned from working with him, as I always do with children, one thing more about my own limitations. I cannot make a difference for every child that is brought to me. And that fact still hurts. Ironic, isn't it? A little boy who thought he was omnipotent taught me that I wasn't.

And I remembered that time he finally relaxed in my arms. He put his little arms around me and laid his hot head on my shoulder. Maybe he will finally let someone hold him, until he, all angles, can unfold.

And I cried. Because it would not be me.

67

Life Is Not All Poop
and Pee

ALLY BUCHANAN, Ana's fellow witch at Halloween, loved to sing and dance and entertain. She had a wonderful time every day with her four other girl friends. She got along with everyone and enjoyed everything we provided. She grew in qualities her parents valued. She was generous, sympathetic, and cheerful. She loved books, could read many words, and loved working with pens and paper, teaching herself the letters of the alphabet. She was constantly asking for instruction as to how to correctly print her letters. And it wasn't always easy to get our attention. She learned how to count to 100 and understood addition and subtraction. I would often watch her teach the four girls the simple concept of six apples, take away three, and "see, Ana, just count how many are left. Now add them back to the pile and they make six again. Pretty neat, huh, Bramble?"

Her parents saw all her academic and social abilities.

They knew she was truly a precocious child. What did disturb them, however, was that their little four-year-old who spoke like a six-year-old would soon be graduating from daycare— and she was still in diapers.

What is more, she was stubborn about it. "No! I don't want to use the potty! I won't do it, I tell you, no!"

Her mother, Maureen, an intelligent and gifted woman, assiduously read *How to Toilet Train Your Child in Ten Easy Lessons* and *Toileting Without Tears* and began her campaign.

"No more diapers, Sally," she said. "You are going to use the toilet. Each time you use the toilet you will get a surprise. Each time you don't, I'll be disappointed and you'll have no surprise."

That didn't work.

Next she tried a "no dessert" policy. But that didn't have any impact either. Then came, "I'll not clean you up anymore. When you poop in those panties, you'll clean yourself up."

During this stressful time, Sally was often angry and sad. Her mother was unhappy too. I told her how miserable Sally had been in daycare, fallout I thought from the toilet training campaign. But Maureen would not back down. She would no longer, as she called it, "ignore the problem." She was certain she would achieve success this time. She read *How to Toilet Train Your Child in a Weekend.*

Frankly, I felt Maureen was losing sight of her daughter in this campaign. But she continued.

She withheld Sally's food after 6:00 P.M., punished her with earlier bedtimes, eliminated TV and bedtime stories.

But nothing worked. She couldn't get Sally toilet trained in a day, a weekend, or a month, with or without tears. And she felt that she didn't have much time left. Meanwhile, the two of them became increasingly distraught.

The truth was, Sally was a sensitive and sweet child. But her resistance to toilet training and her parents' continued insistence on it caused their entire household to turn into a battleground. Toward the end, it left them all feeling exhausted and hurt. Finally, they were able to accomplish urine training, but bowel training seemed not to be.

One morning Sally came to me out in the yard, looking more like her old self. "Joanie," she said, "I'm not going to have any trouble about my poo poos." She looked relieved and happy as she ran off with Ana to join the other girls.

I thought, "Great. She has finally come to terms with the potty."

The next few days she went along just as cheerfully. Her parents became even more cheerful. I assumed that they had finally achieved what they set out to do. But after a few days, Maureen called me aside and asked, "Is Sally having her BMs here?"

"No," I said.

Maureen said that Sally had not had one at home either. She figured out that Sally had not had a BM for four days. She had complained of a stomachache the night before, and, I realized, she had been passing gas during the day.

Sally indeed had found a solution to her problem. She had resolved not to have them anymore.

But, at first, the seriousness of the situation didn't sink in. The next morning I remembered Sally's relief about where to put her poo poos and I called Maureen at work and told her about my conversation with Sally at the beginning of the week. She was frightened and called Sally's doctor, who said to bring her in, wanting to see her right away. By late morning, Sally was flushed and running a slight temperature. The doctor prescribed a children's laxative and, hearing the whole story, suggested that Maureen back down at this point and encourage Sally to let her bowels move into a diaper if necessary.

If the laxatives didn't work, he would prescribe suppositories. An enema would be next. And if that didn't work, the hospital.

Maureen didn't bring Sally in the next day. She called, though, saying that she felt horrible about how this had all turned out. She had used fairly strong methods in dealing with Sally's resistance because she was going on five years old. She simply couldn't accept the fact that Sally was still in diapers. Now she felt trapped. She still didn't want to be lenient with Sally, but at the same time, neither did she want her child in the hospital with impacted bowels.

I empathized with Maureen. To Maureen, her "failure" to toilet train Sally at a certain age meant that there was something desperately wrong with her parenting or with Sally. Both possibilities were equally unbearable.

When toileting is allowed to happen naturally I find that it is as challenging and satisfying to a child as taking that first step or speaking and finally being understood. The expectations for these three skills are all equally clear to a child. The motivation, of course, is that adults and children walk, talk, and use the toilet, so the toddler wants to also.

When parents accept this about toileting, their child has the opportunity to approach this new skill when he or she is interested in doing so. When we see the interest, we assume the child is ready to learn how to do it. When children are approaching mastery of something new, they already have the expectation that they will be successful. Consequently, they can tolerate frustrations and surprises because they know they will achieve the skill. They'll do this without a sense of failure over the difficulties of not always making it on time. The ability to try and try again is simply built into the experience.

Adults in charge are the source of the feelings of failure at home and at daycare. Knowing this, we become *only* facilitators, a resource, in a child's plan, to call upon when needed to take orders. "Pull down my pants, quick! Take me to the toilet. I have to pee *now!*"

While we, as parents or providers, may not always be able to act quickly enough and a child may get angry with us, we both know that this is not our job. We don't assume responsibilities that are the child's alone. We don't initiate and we don't take credit; we just support.

Sometimes it's not convenient for us to drop everything and rush a child to the toilet. While this may cause a frustrating and wet moment, it also says to the child that this is not catastrophic.

It keeps toileting out of the realm of "The Most Important Task in One's Life," which is comforting if there's pressure about it elsewhere. The attitude that sooner or later this will be accomplished is a way of saying to a child, "Relax, you're doing fine. Everything's right in your world. Life is just not all poop and pee."

68

The Five Little Girls
Make Christmas in July

ELL, ANA. Ana and her friends helped cheer me
up after Jason left. These five girls played out
every single thing that was on their mind all
the time. One day during the summer, not long
before they too would leave daycare, Ana and
her four friends asked if they could wrap up all the toys and
give them to the other children when they woke up from
nap.

I thought, "Oh my heavens . . ."

"Oh. We know what toys they'll want!" Ana said.

"They'll know it's just a game, Joanie!" Sally said.

"And they'll love it!" Mary cried.

"Pleasepleasepleaseplease!" said Meredith, tossing her
yellow curls.

I had all of these rolls of wrapping paper from last year.
And I knew right where they were, so I said, "You're going

to have to do this all by yourselves because I'm not going to do it!''

"Oh, we will, we will!" Mary cried.

"I promise you!" Ana said.

This was Ana's idea, of course, so typical of her—spreading cheer in July. Let's give everybody *everything*.

Barbara was taking a nap with the rest of the children. And I was alone with the five girls. So I got all the wrapping paper out and collected the Scotch tape from the basement. Lots of it, because I knew they would pull out a foot or two before it would cut off and they would be stuck with all this tape. But they were good at helping each other. So as I left the kitchen I said, "Okay, this is your thing—don't call me!"

I went to my desk in the other room and every once in a while I'd see Ana or Mary tiptoe past me and run into the small playroom to get the toys and run back into the kitchen where all this furious wrapping was going on.

When it was about twenty minutes before the children were to get up, I peeked my head into the kitchen and asked, "How are you doing? How many more presents do you have to go?"

"Well, we've got Danny and Barney and Crissie and—"

I saw that they were really close so I said, "Twenty minutes left."

They got frantic. "Have we forgotten anyone?" Ana asked. So I went down the list because by this point I was in it too. I didn't want anyone left out either.

"Derek?"

"Yes!"

"Joel?"

"No—oh quick," Ana said and Bramble ran past me out to the playroom to get another toy.

At last, they went rushing into the playroom carrying all the presents, laughing and giggling, terribly excited. They got all their presents piled in the corner of the playroom just in time.

"Shhh." The plan was that we would all hide and then all together we would come out. So we did. Then I thought, "What if all the little ones are disappointed?" But then I thought, "Forget it, Joan. Let them do it and see what happens."

Barbara came into the small playroom with the rest of the children. Half sleepy, still holding their teddies and blankets, they suddenly realized what was going on. Presents! Christmas! There was wrapping paper everywhere as the children dove into the pile of gifts on the playroom floor. They were all so excited. "Look, I got a truck!" "I got a bear!" "I got the sewing bag!"

There was no sense that this toy was now "mine from my house." It was a game and they understood games. But for the five little girls who wrapped them all up, it was as real as Santa Claus. It was about kindness, and giving, and making magical things happen. And, more, the ability to make them happen.

Afterward, they put everything back and felt wonderful for they knew the other children had loved it.

The next day Barbara went into the main playroom with the little ones for naptime and the five girls came in the kitchen and Sally said, "Joanie, we cleaned up everything and we want to do it again."

I looked at her. I wanted to say no, but then I thought, "Let them experience it." So we got out the wrapping paper and the Scotch tape and began all over again.

"But I want to wrap that one this time," Bramble whined. "You said . . ."

"I did not. I am in charge of wrapping fire engines!" Meredith pushed Bramble's hand away and tossed her curls. "Yesterday Joel said—"

"I won't!" Mary told Ana.

"But you have to—" Ana said.

"No, I don't."

I heard all this from the other room. So I went into the kitchen and asked, "How are you doing?"

"Terrible," Bramble pouted. "Meredith won't let me wrap the fire engine."

"She doesn't do it right!"

"Well," I said. "What do you think? You did it once and it worked real well and now—"

Bramble said, "Yeah, it's not any fun."

"I betcha that's why it only comes once a year," Ana added. They all looked from one to the other and reluctantly put everything away.

69

The Five Sassy,
Brassy Vandals

COME SEPTEMBER, our five oldest girls would be going on to kindergarten and their parents were busily searching for the right schools for them.

Sandra, Meredith's mother, decided to bring her own mother to visit us. She wanted her to see that this was a wonderful place for Meredith. And of course, underneath it was a way to get her approval that she was indeed a good mother. So she was showing her around, and of course Meredith was the star, climbing and hanging from everything. But then, when it came time to go, Meredith suddenly ran over and clung to her mother, crying, "Oh, Mommy. Don't leave me." She hadn't done this since her first few times here $2\frac{1}{2}$ years ago.

When they left, I told Meredith, "You little fink."

The five girls had leaving on their minds. As a group, they began to raise hell and defy authority. They hid all twelve

271

of our pairs of scissors. We didn't find them for three weeks. Once they shut themselves up in the bathroom and refused to come out. They sabotaged Hildegard, our music teacher, singing wrong words to the songs in their loudest voices and disrupted play-drama with silly improvisations. Separately they weren't very tough, so they spent most of their time as a pack, bouncing off to the backyard, scheming their next mischief. Usually whatever it was, though annoying, was not too disruptive. But sometimes it went a step or two beyond.

One afternoon while the younger ones were at nap, the five sat at the kitchen table drawing with felt marking pens. Though I was on the phone in the next room, I could hear their chatter. When I hung up and returned to the kitchen, I had a colorful surprise.

They had taken the felt out of the markers and ink was everywhere—in the fruit bowl, on the stools, all over their hands and everything they had touched.

I was furious. "What are you doing?!"

"Well," Ana said, "you see, we are trying to put these colored parts back into the pens and it's hard, isn't it, Mary?"

"It sure is. These aren't made very well, Joanie. I think they just are not good markers."

"They were just fine thirty minutes ago," I said. "I think they aren't made to have the felt pulled in and out."

"Well," Mary said, "they should have been, huh, Sally?"

Sally: "Can I wash my hands now?"

"No," I said. "First clean up this mess. Put all the pens and their insides—"

"Guts! You mean guts!" Bramble laughed.

"Their *insides* in the trash, Bramble, Mary, Ana, Meredith, and Sally!" I looked straight at them. "I'm really upset about this. I can't believe you thought you weren't ruining all our pens."

"Well, you see," Ana said, "Bramble knew but we didn't. Right, Meredith?"

"Right."

Sally, dumping pens in the trash: "Can I wash my hands now?"

"*No!*" I said. "Really, Sally, I am not very concerned about your hands when I see the condition of the table and the fruit bowl and your clothes." I turned and faced them. "All of you! How are we going to clean this up?"

Bramble said, "I am going to do something quiet now," and she left the room.

"Come back here, Bramble. You're not walking out on this."

"I don't like you when you're mad," she said, but she came back to the table.

"Well, how do you think I feel about this?"

She looked up at me solemnly. "Mad."

"I am mad. And I'm not going to get over being mad until this mess is cleaned up."

I gave them soapy washcloths and told them to clean the stools, table, and bowl and to call me when they were done. I would be at my desk. Then I turned and left the room. After a few minutes of quiet, I heard them giggling so I went back in. This time they had succeeded in diluting the colors into pastel hues, but the ink was spread everywhere now.

Sally: "Do you think this will come off my hands when I wash them?"

"You should see your face," I said, feeling mean.

"Look at your face, Ana," Mary said.

"Do I have marks on me like Sally?" Ana said, startled.

"All over you. Hahaha!"

"So do you, Mary," Ana said, wiping her face.

Sally: "We should never have done this. It will never come out even if we wash our hands."

Bramble, still laughing about Sally and Ana's faces, commented, "I think it was fun!"

Sally sat down on a stool. "Help us, Joanie," she said, starting to cry. "I am going to get in trouble if I don't get this washed off."

"I am helping." I had collected all the washcloths and was wiping up the smears.

Sally, still in tears: "But what about my hands?"

Bramble: "It's your face that's bad! Hahaha!"

"Come here, Sally," I said, softening. "I'll wash you."

All the girls piped up, "Me too!" and crowded around. "That's the best I can do for now, Sally, but don't worry. It will wear off."

I continued washing each girl and talking to them as I did. "This is really a mess and that's the end of all our markers until I can get out to buy more. I am feeling better now that we are almost cleaned up but I'm thinking it's a drag not to have drawing pens for the next time we want them. I also need to know from each of you whether or not this might happen again if we get new ones."

"It might," Bramble said.

"Ana?"

"I don't know."

"Sally?"

"It won't. I don't like it all over me."

Mary said, "Well, I don't care if we have markers or not, because I am going to a new school."

Bramble, agreeing, said, "Yeah. Me and Ana and Mary and Sally are going to a new school in September."

Meredith very loftily concurred, "Right. And I am moving far way."

Mary summed it up, "So we don't care."

I sighed, saying, "Somehow September seems very far away. . . ."

That afternoon, one by one, the mothers arrived and asked, "What in the world were you doing?" "What's all over you?" Five times I described the marking pens episode and explained that we had cleaned up as best we could. "I hope it washes out," I said to Sally's mother as she eyed her daughter's brand-new skirt. Sally stared at me, large-eyed. Her mother said, "I think it will."

But it also gave us a chance to talk about what leaving

this place meant to these five little girls, and how they were feeling and acting out their feelings. Our conversations got me thinking.

The next morning, instead of reading a book as usual, I sat down by the fire and announced, "I would like to tell a story about me when I was a little girl."

"How old were you?" Ana asked.

"I was $4\frac{3}{4}$ when my father and mother decided to move to Albany, New York. 'What is Albany, New York?' I asked my mother. She told me it was a wonderful place with trees and hills and that we could visit New York City and see the Empire State Building, the tallest building in the world.

" 'Will we go to the top?' I asked them.

" 'Sure,' my mom and dad said. 'We'll take an elevator to the top and look down on the whole city of New York.'

" 'And have candy?' I asked.

" 'Oh yes, we'll have lots of candy.' They also told me I would go to kindergarten in Albany and play with children my own age and make new friends.

" 'And have a new teacher?' I asked them.

" 'Yes.'

" 'Can't I just have the same teacher?' I asked.

" 'No. Mrs. Mirchindale isn't moving to Albany, New York, and besides she doesn't teach kindergarten. A very special teacher, a kindergarten teacher, will be your teacher.'

" 'Will I like her?'

" 'You will like her.'

"So I was excited to move. My mom and dad brought boxes and we packed our things in them because a big truck was coming to take our things to Albany, New York.

"One morning, a few days before the truck was to come, I stood in my backyard and I realized that I didn't want to have someone else living in my house, swinging in my swing, playing in my sandbox, sleeping in my room. I knew a family was moving into my house because I saw them when they came to look at it. So I went to the kitchen and got a big knife. I wasn't supposed to do that. I wanted it to cut the rope on my swing, but I couldn't do it because the rope was too hard. My mother came outside and took the knife away.

"When I was going to bed that night I began peeling, little by little, pieces of wallpaper off the wall in my room. When I realized what a lot I had peeled off, I was worried and tried to think of a way to hide the damage. I got pieces of paper and tried to glue them to the spot, but it just looked worse so I took them off and had a big, gluey mess. I was worried. I went to my parents' room to tell them I was sorry that I had done it. My mother was sleeping but my father was still reading. He wanted me to whisper so my mother could still sleep, but when he realized I had a lot to say, he got out of bed and we went to my room to talk.

"Right away he saw what I had done. He didn't like it one bit and he looked angry. I started to cry because I thought I made such a big mess that maybe even he couldn't fix it. But he picked me up and held me on his lap. He asked me about the knife and the swing, and about breaking the sand sifter that we were leaving behind. I looked at him. I had forgotten about that. He said that maybe peeling the paper off my wall was the same thing. He told me how he knew it was hard for me leave so much behind and maybe that's why I wanted to mess everything up before I left."

All the children were interested in the story, except for the two youngest. But Ana, Meredith, Sally, Mary, and Bramble were fascinated. I asked if they thought my father was right. The five told me they *knew* he was.

The next month at daycare had its ups and downs. The girls' parents reported some wet beds, food fights, and a few cases of destruction like we had seen here. We were all managing with five very sassy, brassy tearful little girls.

Mary's mother said to us, "I'm glad we decided on kindergarten for this year. Mary has outgrown this place. She says she's bored and how impatient you've become. It sure happened fast."

And Ana's mother commented, "If this is separation anxiety I sure hope it will be over with by the time she gets in her new school. I'm having terrible anxiety leaving here too, Joan, but it's only sadness, really. Ana, however, seems to be hateful.''

I wondered myself, what more do they have to do to leave?

One morning I organized a play. We would all pretend we had been to kindergarten and were coming back for a visit at Joan and Barbara's. The five vandals acted out their disdain for the place. How babyish everything is! How grown-up they are and how the little ones are always in the way. The play wasn't much fun, so it quickly disintegrated. So much for that.

Four of the girls were starting the same school on the fifteenth and Meredith was moving to the Midwest on the tenth. We decided to have one celebration with a cake on the fifth.

"This is it?" Mary said.

"No ice cream?" Ana asked.

"I wish we had balloons," said Meredith.

"Can't we go to Disneyland?" Bramble asked.

I took the opportunity to tell them that we were going to have a special Christmas party for them and for the older ones who had gone on before. So we all had fun making great plans for the future. None of us could stand the present.

PART FOUR

Roots and Wings

70

Off to Kindergarten

FOUR MONTHS LATER, I received a call from one of the two team kindergarten teachers where the four local girls had gone. "Joan," she said, "I just want to know one thing. What in the world do you expect of your kids?"

"Marney, what's up?" I asked.

"When your kids come in the morning, what do you expect them to do?"

"What do you mean?"

"I can't get your kids to sit down in a circle for Show and Tell."

"What do you mean, you can't get them to sit down?"

"Mary, Bramble, Sally, and Ana will sit down for three minutes, and if they're not talking, they're not interested in what somebody else is saying."

"How long is this circle time?"

281

"Well, thanks to them, it's getting shorter and shorter but it's supposed to be about thirty minutes."

"Well," I asked, "do you find it an exciting time? Are you interested?"

Marney said, "Well, not necessarily, but I think every child should have a chance to speak and say their thing."

I was silent. I knew Marney and Christine to be fine teachers, that's why I had supported the parents in sending them there, and I understood her point. But I didn't really agree with her philosophy. At our daycare we believe every child should be heard every minute. We don't carve out one certain time when a child gets to tell something. I think teachers try to structure these kinds of natural occurrences like "sharing," because then we can get them over with and get down to what it's really about which is usually the teacher's program.

Marney continued, "What are your expectations, Joan? Do you ever make them do something they don't want to do?"

"Well," I said, "I don't think I'd make them sit down for thirty minutes if they weren't vitally interested in what they were doing. That amount of time at five years old seems like a lot to me."

Two months later, Marney called again. "I want to tell you that these four girls are amazing. Those kids who were sitting still and minding their own business are now sort of floating around. But your kids are curious, they take care of themselves. They have a fit when we make them clean up other people's messes so we changed that. It made sense to us to no longer have the whole classroom clean up the entire classroom. We have each child be responsible for what they did. Your kids have taught us that.

"All the girls know how to read. And I've noticed, Joan, that if we treat them well, they'll treat us well. Christine and I have to earn their respect, it doesn't just come with the job."

Christine and Marney's class at Redwood School is one of the most permissive schools our children go to. Some of our children, on the other hand, have gone on to Butler School, one of the most academic schools in our area. Not only do they want to know what you do for a living but they ask what your firm is. They reassure parents by saying, "Your child will always be one grade ahead of public schools." We now have on our waiting list a teacher from Butler who wants his two-year-old to come to our place. After our children had been there a while the principal asked their parents for our telephone number because he felt our daycare was a perfect preparation for Butler.

Except for those families we knew in our very earliest years and those few, like Meredith's, that have moved from our area, we are in touch with those children who went to daycare here. They have gone on to academic schools, developmentally oriented ones, and all varieties of other private and public schools. Without exception they have done well in school. I think I know why.

After three years of success they are full of good feelings about themselves and others. They expect to be treated fairly and to be well liked. They are prepared to trust and like the adults and children they meet. So they arrive at kindergarten with their hearts wide open, ready to learn and grow.

I have had this same experience myself as a caretaker when first meeting a two-year-old. Those little ones who have gotten just what they've needed communicate with just a look into my eyes the expectation that I will love them and will treat them well. And I do.

Those children who have survived on, what is for them, a maintenance dose of understanding and emotional nurturance are different. They have developed techniques to be seen and heard. They plead, whine, have tantrums, cry at the slightest frustration, grab from others, defend by becoming the aggressor, and allay their own fears by frightening others. I say, hurrah for these behaviors, because by them they act out for us just what they need. Their unreasonable demands for things are only demands for love and acceptance. Because children are so little and need us so much it is the least we can do.

The child who is indulged with love and family resources is not the spoiled and greedy child many still think abundance brings about. It is the settled and generous one whom everyone likes. This child is not needy for he has reserves. It's like putting money in the bank. This child is brimming over with resources to call upon. He or she will use them to weather the storms in his or her young life. If someone hurts him, he recovers quickly and goes forward with optimism. He is hopeful and resilient. He can love us because he loves himself. He loves himself because another has loved him unconditionally. Nothing has been withheld that nurtures. He has everything. He has learned that he is lovable and so he *is* lovable. We can say this child's needs have been met.

Four months later I attended Redwood School's spring program. The kindergarten and first grade performed a complicated, entertaining routine. very well. I complimented Christine and Marney on their program and asked them, "How's circle time working out?"

"Oh, we found it very frustrating as the other children followed our four little girls' lead. So it's ended up they just assemble every morning in a circle to say hello and begin the day. Sharing time is organized for those children who have something to share. It's no longer mandatory."

I smiled.

"Those four, by the way, are very good students and delightful to be with. In the beginning it looked like the others who had been trained to do what they were told were our best students." She smiled too. "As it turns out these four girls really shine."

71

Jennifer Comes to Visit

'LL BE VISITING MY DAD this weekend. Since I'll be here, can I visit you on Friday?'' Four years later, Jennifer, now age nine, was back for one of her visits. Every three or four months, she would come to visit. She was in the fourth grade at Miss Pringle's, a private girl's school.

"Sure, I want you to come!"

"All day or just half day?"

"All day!"

On Friday, Jennifer arrived with plans ready. "I'll make snack, read for an hour, and teach some French, if you'll let me." Often our older children come back and show us their new skills, and like the proud grandparents we are, Barbara and I love to see them. "Do I get paid, like last time, for working?"

"Sure."

"Is it still two dollars for the day?"

"Two-fifty," I said. "With French." I went over to one

285

of Ana's little brothers, Torey, who was crying, and picked
him up.

Jennifer followed me, saying, "You know, you don't do
enough to prepare these kids for school."

"You weren't prepared?" I asked, as I sat down and
began rocking him in the rocker.

"Well, my school is very demanding."

"Yes," I said, as I got up to get Torey a bottle. Jennifer
followed me into the kitchen.

"But my school is probably more demanding than their's
might be."

"Probably true," I said, as I poured apple juice into the
bottle.

"Yet they really should know *something*, no matter
where they go, you know."

"What would you have them know?" I carried the bottle
back into the playroom. All around us the other children were
skipping, laughing, playing house, reading books. I sat down
in the rocker with Torey in my arms.

"It would be very nice if they knew some reading and
math, Joan. And sitting still. That was very hard for me when
I left here."

I smiled.

"You never make anyone sit still," Jennifer said emphatically. "So how can they get interested in learning?"

"I don't know how to do that."

"That's silly. Anyone can do that. Can I teach them some
just beginning things?"

"Sure."

I then watched Jen spend a very frustrating half hour
with several of the little ones. They had a great time doing
just what she wanted them to do, only doing it *their* way.

She finally came over to me.

"You know," she said with frustration, "they just don't
understand plain English. You have to keep saying the same
things over and over again."

I nodded.

"I don't think they know they aren't doing things right," she said.

"Yes."

"But it is an important job, it needs to be done," she said emphatically.

"What?" I asked.

"Teaching them to *sit still.*" And she went back to try again.

I smiled to myself as I watched her go.

"You do your job," I thought, rocking Torey. "And I'll do mine."

72

"I Wish I Was at Joanie and Barbara's!"

CHILDREN HATE PAST THINGS being brought up. I remember being with my parents in a roomful of people and my mother saying, "Remember, Joanie, the time you—" I'd cringe and know I'd be embarrassed. So whenever I'm with my daycare graduates I don't bring things up. But one time I was up at a cabin with Mitch, now eleven, when his mother asked, "How's Sara's mother doing?" And we started talking about her. And Mitch said, "Sara? I can barely . . . wasn't she the one I used to get in trouble with all the time?"

Sara. I still see her dressed in Mitch's jeans and striped shirt, her face painted like a prince. Sara. Today she is a beautiful twelve-year-old, already an accomplished actress, happy and powerful in her world. She survived that terrible shock to her self-esteem when Mitch left her for a new friend.

While we were at the cabin together, we decided to play Rook. Mitch was looking on and listening so his mother taught him how to play. When he caught on, she went off to read. Every once in a while he'd ask her help, but fairly soon he was playing his own hand.

When he became my partner, I said, "Well, Mitch, let's you and me beat the socks off your dad and brother. There's no reason why we can't win."

"Okay, okay," he said excitedly, moving up and down in his chair. He still wore striped shirts but they were sweat shirts now.

I said, "Don't be nervous, you're doing really well and we're just going to beat them." And we started winning every hand until finally, his father said, "This is not right."

Usually for me, a game's a game, but I was so delighted with Mitch's great judgment. It's a bidding game, and when you get a hand you bid, and you either make the points or go down. Well, Mitch was so excited with this one hand he had. Since I had the Rook, I knew we were going to make it too. This little boy had the bid, and he bid his suit which he wasn't strong in, so he kept hoping to pick up something from the pile. But I wasn't worried because I had everything. It was like somebody dealt me the hand I had always wanted. I kept smiling at him encouragingly and he finally won.

He jumped up and down and I did too.

His father said, "I don't know if you are more obnoxious when you're losing or when you're winning, Joan."

And I said, "Listen, this is a great win. We won this game fair and square. Mitch just learned how to play, you know, and here we are the best Rook players in the world, there's no doubt, so don't give me that bull, you know?"

I left before they did because I had to go back to work that Monday. When it was time to say good-bye, Mitch gave me the biggest hug. And he said in front of his father and brother and everyone, "I love you so much." And I said, "I love you too." And as I held him I wondered if he remembered when he was three years old and he used to say to me, "I love you and I hate you, Joanie."

Eleven-year-old boys don't say, "I love you, Joanie,"

even if they win at Rook. And I think he said it not just because we won at Rook but for all the years he doesn't even remember . . .

Not too long ago, I was in the local copy store when Frank came up to me all flushed and excited. "Joan, I was going to call you on the phone and tell you this because you're not going to believe it. Danny was voted the most popular boy in his class!" He smiled. "I'm not going to quarrel with the fact that they still do that stuff. I'm just so happy it was Daniel."

I laughed.

"My boy!" he said as he happily Xeroxed some yellow tracing paper with sketches on it.

I thought as I looked at him that perhaps both he and Danny have found out that they are enough.

Our graduates continue to use us in many ways. Years after their daycare experience, they call to say hello, they visit, and they talk about us with their families and new friends. As their lives get more complicated I think we stand as a reminder of earlier days when they were learning and experimenting and the consequences were simple and not fearful.

When Jeffie was nine, years after his experience with Greeney, he had one of his first big heartbreaks: he didn't make the baseball team. He asked his mother right then if they could stop by, for he was still wearing his baseball uniform when he arrived. And as he walked in the first thing he said was, "Where's Sandy?"

I smiled sadly and said, "She died, Jeffie."

"Oh," he said and he walked around the playroom.

And I remembered Jeffie at four gathering up a few

books, calling, "Here, Sandy." She came. "Sit, Sandy." She sat. "Lie down, Sandy." And when she obediently laid down, he pushed her gently over to her side, moving her legs just so, making room so he could lie with his head resting on her middle. Then he read his books. Sandy didn't move.

His mother and I had a good visit in the kitchen as he slowly walked around our place. She told me how Jeffie had just spent two years playing Dungeons and Dragons alone in their basement. At first she felt she would be a better parent if she lured him away. But then she remembered Greeney, his shark, and she left him alone. Jeffie emerged from that solitary play accomplished and ready for the world. Nancy said, "Jeffie found a way to do what he needed to do on his own."

As we talked, Jeffie went outside, walked up and down the deck, came into the playroom, and looked at all the books and toys. And then they left.

I know what this feeling is. It is ageless. I have it about my own parents and my own childhood. It is the feeling I have when I find myself wondering, Well, what would Dad think about that? And I laugh at myself because it feels like he's right there with me. But that was forty years ago. We need to preserve safe sanctuaries, these islands of childhood, as one writer calls them.

Tina Washburn, eight years old, was working on her tedious and exhausting piano lessons at home. She has a high standard of excellence and drives herself to perfection. In the kitchen, her mother heard her moan, slam the keys, and at the top of her lungs yell, "I wish I was at Joan and Barbara's!" And then, with calm control, the beginning notes of a song.

Epilogue

A Special Christmas Party

I COME DOWNSTAIRS. It's very early Christmas morning, before Barbara is even awake, and before my four children and nine grandchildren arrive. The house seems huge. The trees outside are bare except for the evergreens, and inside a great tree blossoms in the playroom, covering up all the toys and books and half the room. Underneath it is a little village. It is very dark as I come into the room. I turn on the Christmas tree lights and watch the explosion of green and red and blue and yellow, silver and gold.

I lay under the tree, on my back, my head exactly at the middle, and alongside me I can see all my children of Christmas past and present, our faces and hearts open to the lights and the colors glistening, and all the multitude of shiny ornaments moving to and fro around us. And I say, "Do you see the blue light, the one just nearest to the green one, about two-thirds of the way up?"

"Yes," the children say.

"Now, just to the right of the green light, do you see almost a rainbow of light on the crystal icicle?"

"Where, Joanie? Where?"

"Just to the right and a bit below the green light."

"Yes."

"Do you see it?"

"Yes, oh yes, we see it! We really do!"

There's a marvelous Christmas book for children called *If Christmas Were a Poem*. One of the last lines is, "I guess the most wonderful thing about Christmas is everything good happens at once!"

I remember when I was a little girl lying under the tree looking up. I would lie there for hours and dream and dream. My daycare children do the same thing. They get under the tree and spread their arms and all their thoughts. They think about every little detail and imagine all the wonderful things to come. And each day they play out all their beautiful dreams.

That's exactly what I believe good daycare is—a place where children can spread their arms and thoughts and dreams.

Children need to be able to daydream, long into adulthood. They need to imagine something, anticipate it, thinking through every little detail before they can do it. Here we let children dream and play and percolate.

If you have a very gentle protected daycare, what is being established at this time will stay with you the rest of your life, just as conversely the absence of it will also be with you. And what you are learning, at least here at our daycare, is that as an individual, you're absolutely important. There is nothing about you that isn't accepted and cherished.

One of the things I like best about Christmas at our daycare is that Barbara and I ask each child what they want, and as well as we can, we get it for them. One year Mary, Ana, Sally, and Meredith wanted blue tutus so we went all over town searching for them. Somebody else will ask for a Cinderella doll and another wants such and such a truck.

I think children who come here feel that it's good to want and wish and hope for things because the wanting and the wishing works. They get what they hope for. And I love supporting them in getting it. That's why I enjoy making Christmas exactly how I've always wanted it to be. For me, it is not so much about the past as it is about how beautiful the present is. And as far as I'm concerned, what makes it wonderful is making it happen for a child.

That's why I love what I do. Creating good daycare is indeed like Christmas. It is a way of filling children with anticipation and dreams. It is a way of giving them a place where everything good has the possibility of happening at once.

"Shut up, stupid, you don't see it, it's not by the red ball!"

"It is too!"

"But where is it, you guys?"

"Move over, Meredith, you're mussing me."

"I won't!"

"But where is it, you guys?"

"I see it! There it is!"

"No, you don't. You're too stupid. I know that."

"Oh, I see it too! Oh, you guys, I really do!"